Strange Bedfellows

Strange Bedfellows

Michael J Rowles

Published by Vivid Publishing
P.O. Box 948, Fremantle
Western Australia 6959
www.vividpublishing.com.au

A catalogue record for this
book is available from the
NATIONAL
LIBRARY   National Library of Australia
OF AUSTRALIA

Contents

Introduction

What's it all about, Ezri?[1]

There are three so-called ***Abrahamic Faiths***. They are, in order of their appearance in history: Judaism, Christianity and Islam. According to the World Population Review for 2023,[2] Christianity is the largest religion with 2.38 billion adherents. Islam is the second largest, with 1.91 followers worldwide, and Judaism is the smallest group having around 14.6 million devotees.

I authored this book for Jews and Christians, because of my sincere love for both groups.

Do I not love Muslims? As individuals, yes. I have met some wonderful Muslim people. But, having lived under Sharia Law in Saudi Arabia for just shy of seven years, I have zero doubts about the diabolical origins and aspirations of

---

[1] Ezri is Alfie's Jewish cousin. If you think that that's an inane statement, I must explain that I have serious difficulty in sticking with purely 'ane' statements. Oh, and while I've got you... To be pukka, there should be a list of abbreviations prior to the actual text of this book, and a list of references cited at the very end. However, when I finished writing it, and especially since it needn't be academically reviewed – I simply couldn't be bothered to include those things. Was that terribly naughty of me? You guys are clever enough to figure those things out by yourselves.

[2] www.worldpopulationreview.com/country-ranking/religion-by-country (accessed 01 July 2023).

Islam.[3] According to Islam, Jews corrupted the **Tawrat** – the revelation given to Moses/Musa and Christians corrupted the **Injil** – the revelation purportedly given to Jesus[4]/Isa. That these allegations are not supported by even the tiniest shred of historical evidence, doesn't seem to matter. Moreover, Islam maintains that the Qur'an – written in the seventh century CE – is the only truly unblemished holy book. It just happens to modify significant historical events in the bible (completed centuries before the Qur'an), subtly discrediting major tenets of both Judaism and Christianity in the process.

I authored this book for Jews and Christians, because Islam dominates the Middle East and North Africa. Within decades, Islam may well hold sway in Europe (primarily through high birth-rates among the Muslim population). It is my personal conviction that, as this pre-eminence develops, Islamic persecution of Jews and those Christians who support them, will intensify. Eventually, the Christian Church will split in twain. A remnant of Christians will continue to support Israel and the Jewish people. The rest will side with Israel's enemies.[5]

---

[3] Acknowledging that Wahhabism is not representative of all Sunni Islam... and then there's the Shi'ites too. Crikey!

[4] Henceforth, I plan to refer to him as **Yeshua**. The name Yeshua, as you know, is simply the name that his parents gave him at birth. Its nearest English equivalent is 'Joshua' – a common enough name in the historical and cultural setting of its day, just as it is in ours. However, my deliberate use of his Hebrew name is an attempt to overcome the presuppositions of my Christian readers who pay lip-service to his Jewishness and to avoid any unnecessary offence to my Jewish readers who have experienced suffering and persecution, specifically in that name – Jesus.

[5] If you find that suggestion outrageous, consider the mainstream Christian denominations that are already supporting the BDS movement (Boycott, Divest, Sanction Israel) which was created to punish Israel for defending itself against terrorism.

If this scenario does eventuate, it follows that Jews and the Christian minority will find themselves as **strange bedfellows**, allies of necessity. The fewer the barriers between us at that time, the more likely will be our mutual respect and support.

Before I go any further, I must make clear the foundational premise underlying the rest of this book:

> *JUDAISM AND CHRISTIANITY HAVE THEOLOGICAL DIFFERENCES THAT CANNOT BE RESOLVED BY ANY HUMAN ARGUMENT*

I authored this book for Jews and Christians, but **not** for the purpose of converting either group to the other's religion.

There, I've said it.

If you don't believe I'm being honest with you – please read no further.

What I will say, however, is that committed adherents of both traditions view their differences as something of an enormous chasm. By way of contrast, I am convinced that our points of divergence, though **real and insoluble**, more closely resemble a drainage ditch, than they do, say, the Grand Canyon. My mission, reflected in this book, is to bring a better understanding and rapprochement to devotees of both faiths.

Why would I want to do a thing like that? Well, here seems to be as good a time as any to tell you a little bit of my story...

I spent the better part of my working life as a military and civilian aviator but have also pastored three Christian churches during that period.[6] It was in 2002, during my first pastorate, that God[7] very clearly spoke to me. He gently, but firmly, told me that my teaching was unbiblical. To say that I was shocked (and just a little miffed) is an understatement. Didn't I uphold scripture as being 'the final authority in all matters of faith and practice (as the old chestnut goes)'? I was as sound an Evangelical Protestant as they come, routinely pointing out the errors of the Roman Catholic and Liberal wings of Christianity. Didn't I also lampoon those greedy money-preaching charlatans on the television? How could God accuse me of being less than biblical?

Nevertheless, over the next few months (extending into years), he began to show me that much of what I taught was simply the 'party line', inherited from the Christian denominations and bible colleges with which I had been associated. I was not a researcher – I was merely a regurgitator who relied heavily on commentaries, textbooks, and the interpretations of those learned and pious men who had gone before me. For the first time, I began to research the scriptures for myself with a mind that was open to alternative explanations, and so began a process in which I systematically examined everything I believed in the light of the bible, without recourse to tradition. As a consequence, I was obliged to discard a sizeable part of what I thought was indisputable truth, when viewed against the backdrop of the scriptures and the historical, cultural, and religious paradigm of Second Temple Judaism. That approach continues to this day, twenty-

---

[6] Definitely not the *better* part of my life! Ask any pastor or rabbi – it sure ain't the easiest job in the world.

[7] I hope it won't cause too much offence to my Jewish readers, if I dispense with circumlocutive words like G-d, L-rd and *Elokim*.

one years later. It has been a rewarding but painful experience, earning me as many enemies as it has friends.

I don't know if my ancestry has anything to do with it, but my paternal grandmother was a Jew. According to Judaism, Jewishness comes from one's mother, so that makes my father Jewish as well. *My* mother was a Gentile and that makes me a Gentile, even though I can trace my lineage back through several centuries of the physical descendants of the patriarchs: Abraham, Isaac and Jacob. Oddly enough, in 1970 the nation of Israel extended the legal 'right of return' to those of Jewish descent, redefined as being the progeny of just one Jewish grandparent. I could have emigrated to the Jewish state on that basis. Well, theoretically, at least.[8]

It's all rather confusing to be honest and raises some awkward personal issues. Never mind Jewish rabbinic law, does *God* view me as being a Jew or does he see me as a Gentile?

Dunno, ask me one about aeroplanes.

But, having said all that, how exactly do I propose to address the barriers that separate Jews and Christians in a way that isn't hackneyed and without being accused of promoting a hidden Christian missionary agenda?

The answer is surprisingly simple. I propose to offend both groups with what I believe to be a few home truths that are worthy of their consideration.

---

[8] I say 'theoretically' because the right of return excludes Jews who have converted to another religion.

No, wait, that's a bit too confrontational.

How about this instead...

Take the Red Pill and see just how far I'm willing to push beyond the boundaries of orthodoxy in my arguments. If at any stage you want to resume normality, take the Blue Pill. You'll forget this ever happened and you'll never see me again.

I authored this book for Jews and Christians, excluding the thin-skinned variety. It isn't an attempt to stimulate fervent religious ire from those on either side who are determined to fall upon their swords over **traditional** — note that I didn't say **biblical** — religious dogma. Remember that my motivation is based on genuine love for both groups, not to spark further counterproductive animosity. Whether you are a Jew or a Christian, if you're not willing to be challenged (that sounds much nicer than 'offended', doesn't it?), please read no further.

You're still here? Good. Let me add that I am a Christian with some understanding of Judaism. I can see clearly the errors in my own religious system, and I shall have no hesitation in addressing them. If I feel that any criticism of Judaism would be helpful, my aim is to restrict it to questions of philosophy or logic, and not any errors *per se* — that's beyond my purview. If there are problems with Judaism, it is for Jewish scholars to address them.

What areas of controversy do I intend to investigate that would be certain to bring offence? At the risk of oversimplification, the rest of this book will primarily be a discussion of three major obstacles — elephants in the room, if you prefer — which have driven the greatest wedge between

Jews and Christians for many more centuries than they should have. If I can navigate a path of least discord between the two groups without pretending that these issues don't exist and provide a better basis for mutual understanding and discussion, this book will have achieved its aim.

That's enough preamble from me. What will be the main topics of discussion in the rest of this writing? In other words, what particular pachyderms in the parlour do I plan to posit for parley?

First Elephant

Photo: Rob Hampson · Upsplash

The first elephant is only a little fellow,[9] and his name is *Elephas Maximus Borneensis.* He is the pygmy elephant of

---

[9] If this were the story of Goldilocks, he'd be baby bear.

Borneo, Indonesia and Malaysia. As well as being the most diminutive of the three, this chap is also (for the purposes of this book) a hybrid elephant. He is comprised of all those ideas that **unnecessarily** divide Jews and Christians. I refer to concepts like the eternal relevance of Torah, the belief in eternal damnation and the popular contemporary thought that the Apostle Paul ruined an otherwise semi-reasonable Jewish religious sect.

The first two are based on Christian error; the third is a Jewish misconception. We will tackle the little elephant first when we get into the main body of this treatise.

Second Elephant

Elephant number two is *Elephas Maximus Indicus*, the Indian jumbo. He's a middle-sized critter, but don't let his stature fool you into thinking that he is powerless. And that's because he's the first of two *non-negotiable differences* between our two camps. He is the Christian belief that Yeshua is the Messiah of Israel.

How can I ever hope to deal with such a divisive issue without losing you, whether you be Jew or Christian, from reading further? In a nutshell: to my Christian readers I say Yeshua did not fulfil the messianic expectations of Second Temple Judaism.

No, Christians, he ***didn't***.

To my Jewish readers I say we are all waiting for the true Messiah of Israel to fulfil all those expectations of Judaism. If it turns out that his name is Yeshua of Nazareth, Christians can say, "I told you so." If, instead, he is Morrie Berkowitz from Bondi Junction, Jews retain the gloating rights.

When we get to the part that deals with this issue, I will endeavour to strike a path that can accommodate both viewpoints.

Third Elephant

Photo: Sam Mann - Upsplash

Introducing *Elephas Maximus Africanus* the big chap who hails from deepest, darkest Africa. He is a picture of the biggest barrier to mutual acceptance between the two faiths. He is the Christian doctrine of **The Trinity**. Judaism is a fiercely monotheistic faith. There is a passage from the Torah, read during synagogue services (often recited with the eyes covered) to emphasise its significance. The first line of the *Sh'ma*[10] is the perfect encapsulation of Jewish monotheism:

Hear, O Israel: The Lord our God, the Lord is one! [11]

---

[10] Hebrew: שְׁמַע *(sh'ma)* is the imperative second person plural of 'hear' – it's not a suggestion, it's a command. While we're here, all transliterations in this book are my own and may not be the same as conventional spellings. For the Hebrew speakers, I tend to prefer the apostrophe to transliterate the sh'va. That's because I cringe every time I hear Christians refer to this passage as the SHEEmer.

[11] Deuteronomy 6:4.

Now it's time to offend my Christian readers...

The doctrine of the Trinity was a direct outcome of Hellenistic logic, developed through inferences found in the Apostolic Writings. It is not *directly* supported by any text within.[12] The history behind its development is intriguing and even understandable, but it is superfluous to our study. Astonishingly, by the fifth century CE, Trinitarianism was so enshrined in Christian thought[13] that, it was declared to be a salvation/damnation issue!

Think for a moment, my dear Christian reader. How can a *doctrinal* issue – that is, intellectual assent to a theological proposition – be the litmus test of worshipping the one true God? I can agree with all the Christian credal statements under the sun, and still be a perverse and wicked man, as tragically attested by various notorious Christian individuals within the last twenty centuries of church history. The true test of a relationship with God is *character*. Specifically, do I live my life in a manner in keeping with his holy commandments?[14]

So, what's to be done about this third elephant?

---

[12] There is one exception called the 'Johannine Comma' which occurs in the first epistle of John, chapter 5, verse 7. The 'comma' was a scribal addition (called a 'gloss') first appearing in a fifteenth century CE Latin translation. It was incorporated in Erasmus' 1522 published Latin-Greek New Testament – but only in its third edition. The 'comma' was not part of the original Greek Apostolic Writings.

[13] Do an internet search for the historic 'Athanasian Creed' if you want more details.

[14] Or to put it in techo terms – *orthopraxy trumps orthodoxy.* Please also note that fine upstanding citizens of other and no religious affiliations will most likely *fail* this test. Inevitably, one or more of the commandments of God will be offensive to, and rejected by, such people. That is to say, that their conduct is 'good' as they and/or their culture defines it; not as God defines it.

My plan is to try and persuade my Christian readers of a more biblical and Hebraic approach to the ontological nature of God. That last statement is likely to cause much harrumphing and slamming of this modest work amid cries of "We found a heretic! May we burn him?"[15] I will present an alternative approach to trinitarianism later in the book, while keeping a beady eye out for the Inquisitors. In the meantime, to my Christian brothers and sisters, I say:

> If you want to believe that there is one God in three persons: father, son and holy spirit, coequal, and eternal... knock yourself out. Who am I to stop you? Just don't make a song-and-dance about it, because you will immediately alienate almost every Jew and Muslim on the planet.

Enough Jumbos, Already – What's the Deal?

Try this for size...

Suppose we can make the little elephant disappear, derived as he is, from misunderstanding. For the Indian Elephant, if my Jewish readers could think of Yeshua as a Torah-observant Jew who claimed to be the Messiah (whether he was or wasn't not being the point); and, as for the big bloke from Africa, if Christians really want to keep their belief in a triune God, despite the profound intellectual (and mathematical) difficulties with that concept, as long as they keep it to themselves...

---

[15] Perhaps there will even be cries of, "He turned me into a newt!" (this statement will only make sense to fans of the Monty Python gang. To those of us who fit into that category I say, watch the footnotes for more! To those who are not I say, I shall pray for you).

Would we be able to get along a bit better?

If the above two suggestions are preposterous to you, then I shan't keep you any longer. So long, and thanks for all the fish. However, if you are willing to have a few cherished assumptions challenged, I encourage you to read on.

I have divided *Strange Bedfellows* into six main parts. In the first part, we'll get all the necessary foundational stuff out of the way. You know, those background concepts that are essential knowledge for the main event. Every training course you've ever done has begun with that kind of thing. What can't be avoided must be endured, like a pre-dinner speech.

The next three parts will present my evidence, briefly stated above, to deal with the elephants in the room.[16] Part five is devoted to an alternate explanation to Christian trinitarianism, and the final section is a brief conclusion to all of the above.

Let's get on with it, shall we?

---

[16] It's a big room, okay?

Part One:
How did We Get Here?

The purpose of this first section of the book, is to try and discover how we got from *there* to *here*. What I mean by that is, how is it that Judaism and Christianity have such divergent views today, given that the latter began as a sect of the former?

It's quite a story, actually.

Before that though, there are some of other issues that I am obliged to discuss. In the first chapter of this section, I want to establish the reference material I have used to present my case and, in the chapter following, I'll speak briefly about worldviews.

By chapter three, I'll start getting into the real issues, beginning with the problems that arise when a Western mindset is applied to Semitic writings. In chapter four I hope to demonstrate to my Christian readers that the Church – sorry, there isn't a polite way to say it – lost the plot. Severed from its Jewish foundations, Christianity diverged significantly from its roots, embracing all kinds of Hellenistic thought and practices. It may be surprising to some of my Christian readers just how swiftly we drifted from biblical truth.

In chapter five, I will discuss the historical events that further served to drive a great big wedge between mainstream Judaism, the sect that declared Yeshua to be the Messiah (they referred to themselves as 'The Way'), and the gentile members that were permitted entry into that early Jewish group (around ten to fifteen years after its inception).

I'm anticipating a smooth journey but, just in case of unexpected turbulence, please keep your seatbelts fastened.

Chapter One:
Reference Use Only

Righto, at the outset of this foundational section, I must establish the texts that I'll be referring to in the remainder of this book. And what better place to start than with the bible – what exactly do I mean when I use that term? The Christian version is fatter than its Jewish counterpart – how can that be so?

The Tanakh

The sacred writings of the *Tanakh* [17] were composed, under the inspiration of God, by physical descendants of the twelve tribes of Israel.[18] Moses wrote the first five books of the Tanakh (contrary to some scholarly ideas).[19] It took over a

---

[17] The Jewish Bible, known as the *Old Testament* by Christians. Jewish and Christian bibles contain the same collection of books/ancient writings but arranged in a different order. The Tanakh arranges the books according to their category. The term Tanakh is an acronym (T–N–K) representing its three main divisions: *Torah, Neviim,* and *Ketuvim,* loosely translated as 'Law, Prophets and Writings'. The final book in the Tanakh is Second Chronicles – one of the 'writings'. The Christian bible arranges them in what was believed to be the chronological order of composition. The final book is Malachi, the last one written. I prefer the name Tanakh because the Christian name 'Old Testament' implies that it is now superseded.

[18] Although, there is a section in the Book of Daniel attributed to the Babylonian King Nebuchadnezzar.

[19] There is a theory in some circles that Moses did not write the Torah. Rather, say these academics, there were four different authors whom they call J, P, E and D. This theory, first expounded in the late nineteenth century by Julius Wellhausen (1844-1913), is known as the *Documentary Hypothesis.* I utterly reject it, in favour of

thousand years to complete the Tanakh, the final book being added during the late fifth century BCE. The Tanakh is written (almost) entirely in the Hebrew language.[20]

Both *Jews and Christians* recognise the Tanakh as sacred scripture.

Torah

For my Christian readers, I will now explain a little bit more about 'the Law' or 'the Law of Moses'. I prefer to use the Hebrew term **Torah,** principally because it is a more precise description than the English word **law.** [21] The Torah is contained within the first five books of the bible (whether published in the Christian or Jewish sequence) and contains 613 specific commandments, called **mitzvot.** [22] The Ten

---

traditional Mosaic authorship. By the way, some say Moses also wrote the Book of Job.

[20] With the exception that, of its 23,000+ verses, 268 were written in Aramaic. Most of them are in the Book of Daniel.

[21] The best translation of the Hebrew word Torah is 'instruction'. Why do Christians refer to it as 'law'? The answer is simple: in the Apostolic Writings, the Greek word νόμος *(nomos)* – a word which primarily means 'law' – is used to translate the Hebrew term תּוֹרָה *(Torah)*. Therefore, Torah becomes 'law' in English. However, of the 200+ examples of *nomos* in the Apostolic Writings, all but two are in reference to Torah. Some may think of this as semantics. But, to show you the difference between instruction and law, consider the last time you bought a television set. If bought new, it came with an instruction manual. This booklet aids the owner in using the TV as the manufacturer intended. That is to say, it directly benefits the owner. If the owner happens to live in the UK, an annual licence fee must be paid by that owner to view television broadcasts on the set. That's **law.** There is no direct benefit to the owner of the television, it's simply the law (and serves that individual right for being a 'pom'). God's Torah was not for his satisfaction, it was given for the benefit of his people.

[22] Ashkenazi Jews say 'mitzvos'. For the remainder of this book I will stick to the Sephardic pronunciations (over Ashkenazi) as being closer to biblical Hebrew.

Commandments[23] given to Moses at Mount Sinai on tablets of stone are a fine *summary* of Torah.

The Torah is the foundation of the entire bible. No other sacred text can *ever* contradict the Torah. Some Christians will baulk at that statement, believing that Yeshua somehow abrogated Torah. I will explain why this cannot be so, a little later.

But wait, there's more…

Oral Tradition

Jews have extra-biblical sources to enable compliance with Torah in their daily lives. Judaism asserts that, in addition to the written Torah,[24] Moses received verbal instructions[25] on how to obey the written Torah. Moses passed on these instructions to Joshua, and they were subsequently communicated to the prophets and sages throughout the generations.

Mishnah

Sometime in the second century CE a publication called the *Mishnah*[26] was produced. It is an ancient record of how the Jewish people interpreted and applied Torah to their

---

[23] Hebrew: עֲשֶׂרֶת הַדְּבָרִים – literally: 'the ten words'.

[24] Hebrew: תּוֹרָה שֶׁבִּכְתָב *(torah sh'bikhtav)* – 'Torah that is written'.

[25] Known as 'Oral Torah' – Hebrew: תּוֹרָה שֶׁבְּעַל פֶּה *(torah sh'b'al peh)*.

[26] *Mishnah* means '[from] repetition' suggesting that it was memorised.

communities. The Mishnah has references to both oral and written Torah, along with debates and rulings on various fine points of law.

Talmud

Rabbinic commentary[27] was added to the Mishnah by about the fourth century CE and the combined writings became known as the *Talmud,*[28] which provides an ongoing reference for Jewish *halakhot.*[29]

Christians do not accept the authority of the Oral Tradition.

The Christian Bit

Now we come to the Christian supplement to the Tanakh, the Apostolic Writings, more commonly known as the 'New Testament'.[30] These were composed in the Greek language between 40 and 100 CE by the first disciples of Yeshua and

---

[27] Called Gemara from the Hebrew גְּמָר *(g'mar)* meaning 'final'

[28] There are two versions: the Babylonian Talmud and the Jerusalem Talmud, named according the location in which they were compiled. The former is larger and considered slightly more authoritative. The word Talmud means 'study' or 'learning' from the Hebrew verb לָמַד *(lamad)*, 'to learn' [For the grammar purists: Hebrew verbs are usually expressed in the third person masculine Qal (simple) forms. For convenience, I will translate them using the English infinitive].

[29] This word is also spelled *halachot* and comes from the Hebrew verb הָלַךְ *(halak)* meaning 'to walk'. It describes the way we conduct ourselves.

[30] I prefer the name 'Apostolic Writings' for the same reason as footnote one – to remove any idea of supersession.

their associates.[31] Contrary to the opinions of some Christians, the Apostolic Writings do not, cannot, and will never overrule or replace the authority of the Tanakh. Rather, they are meant to complement the Tanakh, and like that older collection, they are comprised of a number of smaller books.

For my Jewish readers, although written in Greek, the Apostolic Writings were all composed by religious Jews[32] living in the historical and religious milieu of the period we call the Second Temple era.[33] The first five books are historical narrative; the final book is a typical example of 'Jewish Apocalyptic' symbolism, like sections of Daniel and Zechariah. The rest of the Apostolic Writings are letters, written in response to specific issues that arose in the various assemblies in the diaspora of the first century CE. They are primarily *halakhic* instructions – guidelines for daily living.

Just while we're on the subject, some like to make a big thing about the 'Christian' pseudepigrapha. Every now and then, a television channel or other similar organisation will claim that the Christian church rejected those 'gospels' that didn't comply with their agenda (to impose control on the hapless populace). There is the Gospel of Peter; the Gospel of Mary; the Gospel of Judas Iscariot(!), and scores more of these

---

[31] As the names of these authors of the Apostolic Writings arise, I will initially introduce them by their historical names – not their popular Anglicised versions. This is to remind my readers that these men came from a Jewish culture, not our Western one.

[32] Two of the Apostolic Writings books were written by a first-century CE physician named *Loukas* (Luke in our English bibles). According to some, Luke was a gentile proselyte to Judaism. Others maintain that he was born a Hellenic Jew. In either case, he would have been conversant with the Hebraic outlook on both life and the *Tanakh*.

[33] The Second Temple period extends from the sixth century BCE until the destruction of the Jewish Temple in 70 CE.

spurious documents. Since the finalisation of the official books of the Apostolic Writings (the Canon) took place in the late fourth century CE, critics have added two and two together, getting five as the result.

The reality is that these writings have always been recognised as gnostic forgeries, written a couple of centuries after the approved books. The Council of Hippo in 393 CE met to establish whether three of the traditional Apostolic Writings truly belonged in the Canon. They applied strenuous tests of authorship and determined that those three books remain included.

A quick perusal of any of the gnostic texts them reveals a total absence of Hebraisms. They are also devoid of any understanding of Second Temple Judaism.

Jews do not recognise the Apostolic Writings as sacred scripture, Christians do.

Odds and Ends

We will also, as necessary, refer to other ancient texts not considered to be authoritative by either group. These documents are not divinely inspired but they do provide invaluable assistance in comprehending the biblical texts themselves. Both Jews and Christians have an abundance of 'secondary-source' documents. We will spend quite a bit of time in extra-biblical Jewish texts, hopefully gaining greater insight into our topic. The ancient Christian patristic texts, replete with archetypal Hellenistic logic as they are, are of more hindrance than value to our exploration. For the most part, we will choose to ignore them.

I will refer to 'biblical' references using the common chapter and verse system, ensuring to differentiate between Tanakh and Apostolic Writings to avoid any confusion. My Christian readers must accept that, to religious Jews, Talmud is an authoritative reference. In a similar vein, I ask my Jewish readers to be mindful that Christians see the Apostolic Writings as inspired scripture.

X

Chapter Two:
I Joined the Navy to See the World[34]

What is a 'worldview'?

Simply put and, as the name implies, it's just the way we see the world. It should come as no surprise that not all cultures have the same concept of how this world we live in works, nor the same philosophy of how best to live within it.

Only about one-third of the planet shares the worldview with those of us who live in western cultures. Broadly speaking, Westerners may or may not believe in God, and it's certainly trendy to be an atheist in this day and age. Nonetheless, if God does exist, most in the West would say that he is out there somewhere and doesn't interfere all that much with what goes on in the world on a day-to-day basis. Of course, he gets the blame whenever humans do something wicked and is a useful talisman when we want something or when we're in deep kimchi. Primarily, though, we in the West rely on scientific knowledge to get us through our daily lives.

That's not how it works with most of this planet's human population. Most folks in non-western cultures embrace an animistic worldview where the spirits (of whatever sort they

---

[34] That's not true, I've never, ever been in the Navy nor, come to think of it, have I ever been a member of the *Village People*. Pity. They wore some... interesting outfits.

may be) interact with every aspect of life and nature. I'm overgeneralising, obviously, but it may be fair to say that reliance on scientific knowledge is not as prominent in the animistic world.

Our worldview is not something we choose. Rather, we subconsciously absorb it from the perspectives and traditions of our host cultures, osmotically, if you like. Our Western mindset isn't inherently inferior to any other culture's perspective, and I would never advocate animism. Nonetheless, as I have discovered, the biblical worldview is different to both major global perspectives.

I don't know if it comes from my Jewish heritage of not, but my journey of understanding has led me to the unshakeable view that the bible must be viewed through a **Hebraic** worldview. The Hebraic paradigm is far removed from animism, but it isn't entirely the same as the western variety either.

I believe that I can demonstrate that the Christian Church, dominated as it has been for the last nineteen centuries of its existence by the Western worldview, will inevitably interpret biblical texts as if they were written by Plato or Aristotle, or even the late Stephen Hawking.

In the next chapter I will endeavour to illustrate the differences between the Western and Hebraic worldviews and how they affect our understanding of the scriptures.

Chapter Three:
Hebrewsmen & Greeksmen[35]

Last chapter, I declared that the Western worldview can be a bit of a liability when trying to understand the bible, with its Hebraic authorship. In this chapter I want to reveal the differences in the mindset, logic and hermeneutical approaches used by Hebrewsmen & Greeksmen groups. This is one of those chapters that some readers may find a little bit too academic for their taste. Feel free to skip to the 'bottom line' at the end of this chapter if it starts to put you to sleep.

In fact, from now on, I think I'll do the 'bottom line' thingy at the end of most chapters for those who find all the details to be somewhat ho-hum.

Mindsets

The Greek mindset is comfortable with **abstract** concepts, seeing no problem with terms like 'anger' to describe an emotional reaction. In contrast, Hebraic thinking can always be reduced to a **concrete** term, something that can be observed

---

[35] A little over thirty years ago, I was strolling through the streets of Athens. In those days I sported a large handlebar moustache – a legacy of my time as an RAAF aviator. Upon observing my hirsute upper lip, a local resident walked straight up to me, pointed his finger at my face and solemnly announced, "You have moustache like Greeksman!" I think it was meant as a compliment and, ever since, I have thought of Greeks as 'Greeksmen'. It seems only fair to afford 'Hebrewsmen' the same dignity. I mean, many Jewish men have facial hair, don't they?

through the five bodily senses. In biblical Hebrew, one of the terms for anger אַף (*aph*) is the same as the word for 'nose', would you believe? That's because when one is angry, one's nostrils flare. It is a condition that is observable through the faculty of sight.

Greek thinking is **descriptive**. Given a pencil and asked to describe it, the Greek thinker will provide details about its colour, length and whether its cross-section is a circle or a hexagon. Hebraic thinking is *functional*. The Hebraic thinker will describe the same pencil as 'something I write with'.

The Difference in Practice

Here's a simple example, taken from the Apostolic Writings, that will demonstrate the Greek abstract-descriptive versus the Hebrew concrete-functional approaches. The text below comes from a series of teachings called the 'Sermon on the Mount'. It was written down by one of Yeshua's earliest Jewish followers, Mattityahu/Matthew:

> *The lamp of the body is the eye. If therefore your eye is good, your whole body will be full of light. But if your eye is bad, your whole body will be full of darkness. If therefore the light that is in you is darkness, how great is that darkness.*[36]

What did Yeshua mean by saying that a person can have a good (or bad) eye?

---

[36] Matthew 6:22-23. It was also recorded in *Loukas'* narrative (Luke 11:34).

Consider this concluding paragraph from an eight-page article exploring this very question. First published in the 1960s in a scholarly journal called *Neotestamentica,* It is a typical representation of Greek thinking:

> The eye played in the ancient near east from the earliest times up to the time of the New Testament in an important role as the representation of human feeling and as the reflection of that feeling. No wonder that the ancient cultures ascribed to the eye magical force. From these magical conceptions certain terminology developed which became a fixed part of the languages of the ancient Near East and which, stripped of its magical meaning, found its way into the [bible].... Jesus linked up with this idea in his maxim about the eye, but true to his message, and in agreement with his usage of well known [sic] phenomena, He especially stresses the effect of the eye on man himself. He also combined the concept of eye with the great contrast between light and darkness and showed the importance of the eye as the lamp of the body.[37]

Dunno about you, but I don't understand the above explanation even slightly, and the preceding pages were no more lucid than this excerpt. Certainly, I would be none the wiser on the subject, were this the only explanation available.

The simple solution to the biblical text comes from knowing that 'good eye' and 'bad eye' were figures of speech in ancient Judaism. To have a 'good' eye was to be a generous person; to have a 'bad' eye was to be an avaricious miser. This is easily proven by reference to other texts in the Tanakh and Apostolic Writings[38] without the need for a lengthy and unfathomable scholarly article. Rather, a familiarity with the biblical texts is all that is necessary.

---

[37] Fensham, F.C., *The Good and Evil Eye in The Sermon on the Mount*, in *Neotestimentica* 1 (1967): 51–58. http://www.jstor.org/stable/ 43048835 (accessed 11 May 2023).

[38] e.g. Proverbs 28:22; Matthew 20:1-16 – the Parable of the Labourers.

What if those explanatory verses from the Books of Proverbs and Matthew were not available? The correct solution would still be attainable through an understanding of Hebraic thought, and its reduction to concrete concepts, wherever possible.[39] To the authors of scripture, 'the eye' was a picture of *wisdom* because the world is viewed or observed through this sensory organ. To have a good eye meant to view the world in a righteous or godly manner; a man who regarded the world with wicked or selfish motives had a bad eye. The quote above is in the broader context of Yeshua's teaching against materialism.[40] Thus, the man with the good eye views the world in sensitivity to the needs of those less privileged than himself. The self-centred, greedy individual sees the world through his bad eye. Unlike Greek-inspired abstract terms: generous and greedy, for example, the word 'eye' in Hebraic understanding gives us a concrete base for interpreting the true meaning of Yeshua's teaching.

Logic

Greek logic is **linear**. It starts with a premise, continuing through a series of logical steps to arrive at the conclusion. Hebraic thinkers are content with **block** logic. That means that they are quite at ease in holding various 'blocks' of ideas in tension with each other, even if they seem contradictory.

To illustrate what I mean by this, Greek-thinking Christian Protestants have divided over the issue of the sovereignty of God and the free will of man in the salvific process. In other

---

[39] More on this later.

[40] The passage is Matthew 6:19-34 in which vv.22-23 are contained.

words, does God choose some to salvation (and not others),[41] or does man offer his life to God of his own free will? [42] Some scriptures provide *prima facie* support for the former, and others the latter. Thus, the Greek-thinker finds himself[43] on the horns of a dilemma. Either he must choose to ignore any biblical text that contradicts his view, or he must apply casuistry – Greek linear logic (at its finest), to prove that the alternative texts, once rightly understood, actually **support** his own presuppositions.

The tragic conclusion of Greek-inspired theology is that Christianity retrogressed into a credal religion. *Orthodoxy* – mere intellectual assent to a doctrinal position – became the decisive test of adherence to the faith, irrespective of one's conduct before God and men.

The Hebraic thinker, with his block logic, is totally at ease holding both sides of a coin simultaneously. God is sovereign and controls the end from the beginning *and* man has free will to choose. The need to resolve this seeming paradox is a pointless exercise because there are far more critical issues at stake. The precise mechanism is of little consequence. Of far greater weight to the earthly-thinking Hebrew, is *orthopraxy* – how does God want us to conduct ourselves?

---

[41] Called 'Calvinism' after its foremost advocate, John Calvin (1509-1564). The Presbyterian denomination is Calvinist. John Piper, author of over 170 Christian books is a highly regarded Calvinist.

[42] Known as 'Arminianism' after Jacobus Arminius (1560-1609) who opposed 'Calvinism'. The Methodist denomination endorsed Arminianism. Rick Warren (1954-), author of the book, *The Purpose Driven Life* which has sold 50 million copies published in 85 languages is a famous Arminian.

[43] For convenience, the use of masculine pronouns in this book is intended to be gender-inclusive, with the specific exception of references to God, where the masculine pronoun is intentionally exclusive. Besides, there are so many different personal pronouns to choose from these days, aren't there?

Hermeneutics

Now it is time to turn our attention to hermeneutical differences. *Hermeneutic* is just a technical term meaning: 'a method or theory of interpretation'. The Greek approach may be divided into two historical methods: the Roman Catholic hermeneutic and the Protestant hermeneutic. The latter arose as a backlash against what was viewed as the impropriety of the Catholic process.

The Catholic Hermeneutic

By the Middle Ages, the Roman Catholic church had developed four levels of scriptural interpretation, as per the table below:

Level	Meaning
Literal	The straightforward meaning of the text
Typological	The allegorical meaning of the text
Tropological	The moral meaning of the text
Anagogical	Prophetic pictures derived from the text of future and final (eschatological) events

An in-depth analysis of these Catholic levels of interpretation would have no relevance for this chapter, except for the second level: the typological (allegorical) level. Using this method, a commandment in the *Torah,* was routinely allegorised to have a different interpretation for the Christian. This approach became commonplace early in Gentile Christian history.

Let me give you a 'frinstance'. The Torah declares some food unfit for human consumption:

> ...[the swine] is unclean to you. Their flesh you shall not eat, and their carcasses you shall not touch. They are unclean to you.[44]

Even by the early second century CE, the (by then) almost exclusively gentile church had adopted this allegorical method. 'Barnabas'[45] lived around 100 CE and describes the allegorical application of the above statute for Christians:

> Now, wherefore did Moses say, "Thou shalt not eat the swine...?" ...Moses spoke with a spiritual reference. For this reason, he named the swine, as much as to say, "Thou shalt not join thyself to men who resemble swine." For when they live in pleasure, they forget their Lord; but when they come to want, they acknowledge the Lord. And [in like manner] the swine, when it has eaten, does not recognize its master; but when hungry it cries out, and on receiving food is quiet again.[46]

---

[44] Leviticus 11:7b–8.

[45] Not the same Barnabas that was Paulos' (Paul's) travelling companion in the Book of Acts. Further details of the Barnabas quoted here are lost to antiquity. The name was most likely a pseudonym.

[46] Robert A. Kraft, *The Epistle of Barnabas: Its Quotations and Their Sources,* http://ccat.sas.upenn.edu/rak/publics/barn/barndiss01.htm (accessed 08 July 2023).

According to the typological method, a simple instruction about diet has been allegorised to mean that 'Christians' should not associate with those who are not spiritually and morally enlightened. What is Barnabas' proof for this explanation?

There isn't any. He simply made it up.

The Protestant Hermeneutic

The Protestant Reformers, with their insistence on scripture only[47] rejected the Roman approach and applied the historical-grammatical method. Essentially, the process involves trying to understand the words, their syntactical and grammatical meaning and the type of literature under investigation, all within the cultural setting in which the document was written. This is the same process that would be applied to any other ancient text.

Rightly repulsed by Catholic abuse of it, Protestantism rejects typology *unless* the bible confirms its validity. For instance, they would see the Passover lamb as a prophetic picture of Yeshua, but only because this *type* is verified in the Apostolic Writings:

> *Therefore purge out the old leaven, that you may be a new lump, since you truly are unleavened. For indeed Christ, our Passover, was sacrificed for us.*[48]

---

[47] Their slogan consisted of five 'solas', the Latin word for 'solely' or 'alone'. They were *sola fide* – faith alone; *sola scriptura* – scripture alone; *solus Christus* – Christ alone; *sola gratia* – grace alone, and *soli deo Gloria* – to God alone the glory.

[48] 1 Corinthians 5:7.

The Jewish Hermeneutic

Judaism also applies four levels of scriptural interpretation.[49] By the Middle Ages, the Jews began to use the word *pardes* as a four-letter acronym representing these four levels. There are only four consonantal letters in the Hebrew word, equivalent to our English letters P–R–D–S. The 'a' and the 'e' added are to the English transliteration based on the Hebrew vowel points.[50] The four Hebrew words and their meanings are as follows:

Hebrew	Transliteration	Meaning
פְּשָׁט	P'shat	'straight' or 'flat surface' – the straightforward meaning of the text
רֶמֶז	Remez	'hint' – comparing similar scriptures to develop a more refined definition
דְּרַשׁ	D'rash	'interpretation' – the symbolic or allegorical patterns
סוֹד	Sod	'secret' – the hidden mystical meaning for those who are skilled in such endeavours

---

[49] Perhaps that's where the Roman Catholic Church got the idea?

[50] פַּרְדֵּס (pronounced par-dace) is a Persian word picked adopted by the Hebrew language during the period of Jewish exile (6th century BCE) under, first the Babylonian empire and later, the Persian empires. It means a 'beautiful garden' or 'orchard' and is the origin of the English word 'paradise'.

The fourth *(sod)* level of interpretation is used in *qabbala,*[51] the mystical form of Judaism which, although a 'dumbed-down' version has been popularised by certain celebrities in recent times,[52] is not recommended for those with less than 40 years of experience in serious Judaic studies.[53] I don't have any experience or understanding of the *sod* level and will not address it any further.

Let us examine a text from the Apostolic Writings, where the first two interpretive levels of *pardes* can be applied. One of the earliest books in the Apostolic Writings was penned by Yeshua's brother Ya'akov.[54]

Writing to Jewish followers of Yeshua in the diaspora,[55] he promises:

> *...he who looks into the perfect law of liberty and continues in it, and is not a forgetful hearer but a doer of the work, this one will be blessed in what he does.*[56]

---

[51] Also spelled kabbalah, cabala etc.

[52] e.g. the singer Madonna

[53] Maybe if I had 40 years of Torah study...?

[54] That is, Jacob. Mysteriously referred to as 'James' in English translations of the Apostolic Writings. There is an urban myth that the translators of the King James (Authorised) Version of the bible appealed to the Monarch's vanity by telling him that there was a book named 'James' in the bible when translated into English. A good story, but there are English translations that predate the KJV and contain the Book of James in the Apostolic Writings. King James, for all his faults, was not a fool that would be taken in by such shenanigans. Another of Yeshua's brothers (he had four) was named Yehuda (Judah). But since the Greek translation of Yehuda is Youdas (Judas) he is referred to as 'Jude' in the Apostolic Writings, presumably to avoid any association with the bad guy Judas Iscariot.

[55] James 1:1.

[56] James 1:25.

What is the 'perfect law of liberty'? Through the application of typical Greek thinking, most Christian expositors somehow see this as a higher law that liberates Christians from the burden of Torah. James was a righteous man,[57] known for his scrupulous observance of Torah and respected by the Pharisees in Jerusalem, despite their disagreement with his belief in Yeshua as Messiah. He had also taken the vow of the Nazirite,[58] totally separating himself for service to the LORD. His nickname was 'camel knees', a humorous reference to the effect on the knees that hours kneeling in prayer would produce. Is it likely, that a man of this piety would encourage his Jewish brethren to 'float above' the Torah? Seriously?

The simple solution is to adopt the second Jewish interpretive stage, *remez,* which looks for hints elsewhere in the scriptures. James' intended meaning is easily determined by reference to David's lengthy psalm which extolls the beauty of Torah.

So shall I keep Your law continually, forever and ever. And I will walk at liberty, for I seek Your precepts.[59]

To walk in liberty means to walk according to Torah! Contrary to Christian interpretation, James is exhorting his Jewish brethren to continue in obedience to Torah (the law of liberty) because there is a blessing in doing so.

Let's now examine the *d'rash* component of Hebraic interpretation. While the Catholic allegorical approach can be

---

[57] Hebrew: צַדִּיק *(tsaddiq).* He is often referred to in ancient Christian writings as 'James the Just', reflecting his Hebrew name: יַעֲקֹב הַצַּדִּיק – *Ya'akov ha Tsaddiq.*

[58] Hebrew: נָזִיר *(nazir).* See Numbers 6:1-21.

[59] Psalm 119:44-45.

employed to make a text say anything you want it to,[60] an allegory drawn from scripture that illustrates another clear, literal (*p'shat*) text is a valid Hebraic technique. It's called *midrash*.[61]

To show the difference between the two methods we will examine Moses' encounter with the Angel of the LORD,[62] who appeared to him in the form of a burning bush:

And the Angel of the LORD appeared to him in a flame of fire from the midst of a bush. So he looked, and behold, the bush was burning with fire, but the bush was not consumed. Then Moses said, "I will now turn aside and see this great sight, why the bush does not burn." [63]

What is the significance of the bush that was burning without being consumed by the flames? The mediaeval Catholic Churchmen said that it was a prophetic picture (a type) of the perpetual virginity of Mir'yam/Mary, the mother of Yeshua.[64] This Catholic tradition is definitely not supported by the Apostolic Writings. Although the gospels do teach that Yeshua was miraculously born of a virgin, they also confirm

---

[60] There is a saying that the bible is like you and me. If you torture us long enough, we'll confess to whatever you want us to!

[61] *Midrash* means literally, 'from *d'rash'* that is, from interpretation.

[62] When we see the word LORD with the last three letters in small caps, it is a circumlocution for the covenant name of God יְהֹוָה (*YHVH*). Nobody knows how to pronounce this name correctly (despite any claims to the contrary). Although this word is accompanied by vowel points in the Hebrew text, they are copied from the word אֲדֹנָי (*adonai*) which (loosely) means 'my Lord'. Their purpose was to remind the reader to say the substitute word *adonai* instead of the sacred name.

[63] Exodus 3:2–3.

[64] Whether these Apostolic Writings texts are true is outside the purpose of this book.

Yoseph/Joseph and Mary had normal marital relations after the birth of Yeshua:

and [Joseph] did not know her till she had brought forth her firstborn Son.[65]

In contrast, I can use *midrash* on this incident in Exodus to illustrate something plainly taught at the *p'shat* (literal) level elsewhere in the bible. I could say, for example, that the burning bush is a picture of the fire of God's righteous jealousy, aroused when he sees his people worshipping false gods:

*Take heed to yourselves, lest you forget the covenant of the LORD your God which He made with you, and make for yourselves a carved image in the form of anything which the LORD your God has forbidden you. For the LORD your God is a **consuming fire**, a jealous God.*[66]

Alternatively, I could suggest that the failure of the fire to consume the bush is a picture of the eternal nature of God:

Before the mountains were brought forth, or ever You had formed the earth and the world, even from everlasting to everlasting, You are God.[67]

The truth is, that I have **no idea** why the Angel of the LORD appeared to Moses in that form. But, unlike 'Barnabas', I have not introduced any spurious extra-biblical assumptions. I have

---

[65] Matthew 1:25. The word 'know' in this text is a reflection of the Hebrew term יָדַע (*yada*) meaning to know experientially or intimately. Here it refers to sexual relations.

[66] Deuteronomy 4:23-24 – emphasis mine.

[67] Psalm 90:2.

merely used an incident from the Book of Exodus to *illustrate* other biblical teachings.

The Protestant Reformers' justifiable rejection of the allegorical method unintentionally threw the baby out with the bathwater, denying *midrash* as a valuable interpretive tool.

The Best Greek Dictionary

As stated earlier, the Apostolic Writings were written in Greek. So, where does the translator, when confronted with an unfamiliar Greek word, turn for definition? Usually to other Greek writings to see how the great philosophers of yore applied the term.

But there's a much better resource than that, The **Septuagint** was a Greek translation of the Tanakh made in the third century BCE.[68] Jews in the diaspora were familiar with the Septuagint and the authors of the Apostolic Writings sometimes cite the Septuagint version of Tanakh texts in their writings.

Given that the writers of the Apostolic Writings were Hebrew-thinking Jews, why do expositors feel compelled to seek word definitions from, say, Aristotle instead of King David?

As it probably says somewhere in Holy Writ:

---

[68] The name 'Septuagint' comes from the Latin word for 'seventy'. That's because it was translated by seventy Hebrew scholars. Its usual abbreviation (LXX) is seventy in Roman numerals.

It does me 'ead in.[69]

What's the Bottom Line?

The Greek approach to the scriptures precipitated four major Christian interpretive shortcomings:

1. The application of Greek, rather than Hebraic, logic results in Christian scholars debating and defending doctrinal issues that have no practical application.

2. The inevitable result was a religion based on creeds and intellectual assent to propositions, at the expense of proper conduct.

3. The rejection of the Catholic allegorical approach to interpreting biblical narrative was the correct thing to do but has denied the validity of midrash.

4. Failure to recognise the primacy of the Hebrew language, elevates Greek philosophical writings to become the 'dictionary' of terms used by Hebraic thinkers who were familiar with the Septuagint.

---

[69] If it doesn't, it should.

Chapter Four:
How the Church Lost the Plot

No shortage of writing exists extolling the Christian Church's triumph over various heretics in its early history. Alas, discussion of the heresies promulgated by the acknowledged Church Fathers and saints is less abundant.[70]

In this chapter, we will investigate a few bizarre interpretations of the plain teachings of the Tanakh and Apostolic Writings. It is intended to be merely a sample. Believe me when I say that, sadly, there is an abundance of such material available.

Creation

One of the first texts in Genesis describes God's creation of the phenomenon we know as 'light':

Then God said, "Let there be light"; and there was light.[71]

The straightforward (*p'shat*) meaning of this verse would be common to Jews and Christians. The difference appears when a deeper level of interpretation is desired. Consider the Jewish *d'rash* meaning:

---

[70] This survey is not intended to call into question the sincerity of these men. Of necessity, though, their erroneous ideas must be considered to complete the task at hand.

[71] Genesis 1:3.

This alludes to Abraham, as it is written, Who hath raised up one from the east, whom He calleth in righteousness to His foot.[72]

Now compare the deeper level drawn from Genesis 1:3 by the second century CE churchman Tatian the Assyrian:[73]

We recognise two varieties of spirit, one of which is called the soul (ψυχή), but the other is greater than the soul, an image and likeness of God: both existed in the first men, that in one sense they might be material (ὑλικοί), and in another superior to matter. The case stands thus: we can see that the whole structure of the world, and the whole creation, has been produced from matter, and the matter itself brought into existence by God; so that on the one hand it may be regarded as rude and unformed before it was separated into parts, and on the other as arranged in beauty and order after the separation was made.[74]

What Tatian's exposition has to do with God's creation of light has totally eluded me.

The Name of God

---

[72] *Midrash B'reshit Rabbah* is a Jewish exegetical commentary on the Book of Genesis written about 250 CE, by the rabbinic teacher R. Hoshaiah. This is a typical midrashic approach in which the Genesis text is used to illuminate another verse of the bible. In this case Isaiah 41:2a which, according to Judaism is a reference to Abraham. Just as the sun rises in the east, so God Abraham from the east - Chaldea (modern Iraq) – to be the one who would rule over kings and nations (Isaiah 41:2b).

[73] Tatian (110-172) was a pupil of Justin Martyr, a famous Christian apologist of the second century CE.

[74] Patrick Healy, *Tatian* in Catholic Encyclopedia, http://www.newadvent.org/Cathen/14464b.htm (accessed 13 July 2023).

Some early Christian errors are difficult to explain. The Tanakh is explicit in stating that God revealed his covenant name to Moses:

Moreover God said to Moses, "Thus you shall say to the children of Israel: 'The LORD[75] God of your fathers, the God of Abraham, the God of Isaac, and the God of Jacob, has sent me to you. This is My name forever, and this is My memorial to all generations.'[76]

Jews do not speak God's name out of reverence, substituting the Hebrew word *Adonai*[77] (loosely 'my Lord') where the sacred name appears in the Tanakh. Nevertheless, the text proves that the name exists and could theoretically be spoken aloud. That is, if the long-lost pronunciation were known.

The early church apologist Justin Martyr (100–165 CE) declared that the name of God could not be uttered at all, even going as far as to say that it didn't actually exist:

For no one can utter the name of the ineffable God; and if any one dare to say that there is a name, he raves with a hopeless madness.[78]

---

[75] The spelling of LORD with the last three letters in small caps denotes that the Hebrew word in the text is the name of God called the 'tetragrammaton'. In English transliteration it is YHVH or YHWH.

[76] Exodus 3:15–16.

[77] As mentioned in an earlier footnote, the scribes added the vowel points of the word *Adonai* to the tetragrammaton to remind readers of the circumlocution. Unaware of this, mediaeval churchmen applied those vowel points to the tetragrammaton and came up with the name 'Jehovah' (in those days, the 'J' had a 'Y' sound).

[78] First Apology LXI.

Resurrection of the Dead

Both the Tanakh and the Apostolic Writings plainly teach the physical resurrection of the dead. Here is an example from the Book of Job:

And after my skin is destroyed, this I know, that in my flesh I shall see God...[79]

Hellenism rejected this concept and saw the final state as being a disembodied existence in a spiritual realm. The Book of Acts records the Apostle Paul's debate with the intelligentsia of Athens. Note their divided response to his proclamation of physical resurrection:

*And when they heard of the resurrection of the dead, **some mocked**, while others said, "We will hear you again on this matter."*[80]

The Apostolic Writings have more references to the physical resurrection of the dead than does the Tanakh. However, the permeation of Greek thought means that most professing Christians believe in an eternal disembodied state, as did the ancient Greeks. Here's an example from 'Mathetes':[81]

The soul is imprisoned in the body, yet preserves that very body; and Christians are confined in the world as in a prison, and yet they are the preservers of the world. The immortal soul dwells in a mortal tabernacle; and Christians

---

[79] Job 19:26.

[80] Acts 17:32 – emphasis mine.

[81] Not his real name. Mathetes is the Greek word for 'disciple' (μαθητής). The real identity of this prolific writer of the second century remains unknown.

dwell as sojourners in corruptible [bodies], looking for an incorruptible dwelling in the heavens. "[82]

Circumcision

God gave physical circumcision of males as a covenant sign between himself and Abraham (and his descendants):

And God said to Abraham: "As for you, you shall keep My covenant, you and your descendants after you throughout their generations. This is My covenant which you shall keep, between Me and you and your descendants after you: Every male child among you shall be circumcised...[83]

Gentiles of the Greco-Roman era did not practise physical circumcision. Incredibly, by the second century CE, some viewed it as being a sign of *punishment* for the Jews:

For the circumcision according to the flesh, which is from Abraham, was given for a sign; that you may be separated from other nations, and from us; and that you alone may suffer that which you now justly suffer...[84]

---

[82] Mathetes, Epistle to Diognetus VII.

[83] Genesis 17:9-10.

[84] Justin Martyr, *Dialogue XVI.*

Mikveh & Baptism

A *mikveh* is a bath or pool in which ritual purification can be undertaken and involves complete immersion in water.[85] The word mikveh means an 'accumulation' or 'collection'. It is found in the following Torah verse:

Nevertheless a spring or a cistern, in which there is plenty of water,[86] shall be clean...[87]

Second Temple Judaism prescribed ritual cleansing in a mikveh prior to entry into the Temple. Sometimes it was also needed to indicate a change in status. A mikveh was part of the process when a man entered the priesthood and women underwent a mikvah routinely at the end of their menstrual cycle. It was an obligatory step in the conversion of a Gentile to Judaism.[88]

Yeshua also stipulated that Gentile converts to The Way to complete this process as part of their conversion:

Go therefore and make disciples of all the nations, baptizing them...[89]

---

[85] Ideally, 'living', that is, running water.

[86] The expression translated as 'plenty of water', is literally a 'collection of water' – מִקְוֵה...מַיִם (*miqveh... mayim*) in Hebrew.

[87] Leviticus 11:36.

[88] Orthodox Jews still see this is a necessity; other branches of Judaism no longer do.

[89] Matthew 28:18a.

Two things are noteworthy in this text. First, the word 'nations' is the Greek equivalent of the Hebrew word for 'Gentiles'.[90] Second, the word 'baptize' is simply an English transliteration of the Greek term meaning to 'immerse'[91] and carries no special religious connotations.

Irenaeus (c.130-202) was an early Christian leader from Lyons. His thoughts on baptism clearly reflect his Gentile heritage, paving the way for the later Roman Catholic position on the supernatural power of baptism:[92]

All waters … after invocation of God, attain the sacramental power of sanctification; for the Spirit immediately supervenes from the heavens, and rests over the waters, sanctifying them from Himself; and being thus sanctified, they imbibe at the same time the power of sanctifying…. Therefore, after the waters have been in a manner endued with medicinal virtue through the intervention of the angel, the spirit is corporeally washed in the waters, and the flesh is in the same spiritually cleansed.[93]

Clothing

The Torah prohibits the blending of certain cloths:

---

[90] The Greek word ἔθνος (*ethnos*) has the same meaning as the Hebrew גּוֹיִם (*goyim*).

[91] βαπτίζω (*batpizo*).

[92] That's why they forced many Jews (and others) to be baptized against their will. Because they believed that the water had supernatural powers (following the correct incantation uttered by an ordained priest), they truly thought they were doing the involuntary baptismal candidate a favour. Sigh.

[93] Irenaeus, *On Baptism IV.*

...a garment of mixed linen and wool [shall not] come upon you.[94]

and specifies that men and women should not wear the same clothing:

A woman shall not wear anything that pertains to a man, nor shall a man put on a woman's garment, for all who do so are an abomination to the LORD your God.[95]

Linen apparel was mandated for the priests[96] but, at no point does the question of cloth colour arise, because:

...for man looks at the outward appearance, but the LORD looks at the heart.[97]

Irenaeus disagreed, seeing purple and sky-blue as being unseemly colours for clothing worn by women:

...for what legitimate honour can garments derive from adulteration with illegitimate colours? That which He Himself has not produced is not pleasing to God, unless He was unable to order sheep to be born with purple and sky-blue fleeces!"[98]

---

[94] Leviticus 19:19; also, Deuteronomy 22:11.

[95] Deuteronomy 22:5.

[96] e.g. Exodus 39.

[97] 1 Sam 16:7.

[98] On the Apparel of Women 1.VIII.

What's the Bottom Line?

The divergence caused by the Christian Church's dependence on Greeksmen thinking contributed to the gap that now exists between Christians and Jews. Cut off geographically and socially from those who already had fifteen centuries of experience in understanding sacred scripture, Gentile Christian leaders applied those methods that were consistent with their Hellenistic worldview, distorting the meaning of the original texts, exaggerating the importance of doctrine while diminishing the significance of godly conduct.

And the rest, as they say, is history.

Literally.

Because certain events in the first few centuries of the Common Era conspired to stretch the breach between Jews and followers of Yeshua, dividing the latter group into mutually hostile Jewish and Gentile believers.

Shall we?

Chapter Five:
Splitters!

Just as there are divisions within Judaism today,[99] there were different sects during the Second Temple era – the Pharisees, Sadducees, Essenes, and Zealots being the four best known.[100] Yeshua's teaching was most in accord with that of the Pharisees.[101] Following the death of Yeshua, his disciples formed a splinter group,[102] referring to their sect as 'The Way', which was, to some extent, accepted by other constituents of mainstream Judaism, as per the diagram below:

---

[99] Orthodox, Reform, and Conservative are currently the three largest groups within global Judaism.

[100] The Apostolic Writings mentions a fifth group called the 'Herodians'. Little is known about them – they may have been a politically motivated group, or perhaps it was a derogatory nickname of some sort.

[101] This may come as a bit of a surprise to Christians, given his frequent and sometimes heated disputes with them in the gospel narratives. Nonetheless, the Pharisees were the religious conservatives of their time, holding the entire Tanakh as inspired and authoritative. They looked forward to a general resurrection of the dead at the last day. The Sadducees were often the wealthier members of the Jewish public, responsible for operation of the Temple and priesthood. They maintained a fragile relationship (purely of necessity) with the Roman occupying forces. They accepted the inspiration of the Torah only and denied any resurrection to come.

[102] No, it wasn't the *People's Popular Front of Judea*.

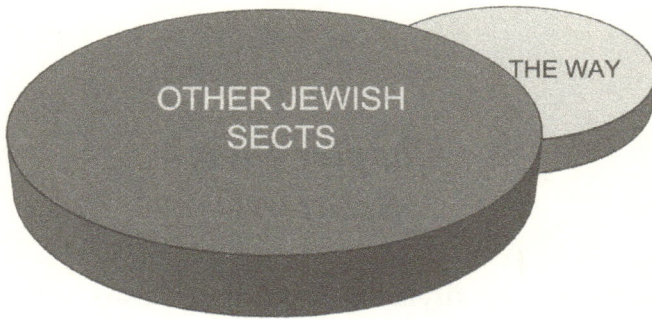

Throughout this period there were always gentiles attending Jewish synagogues. While a minority did undergo a full proselyte conversion to Judaism,[103] most opted to remain as gentiles. A gentile worshipper was known as a 'Godfearer' in Greek[104] or, in Hebrew, a 'foreigner-sojourner'.[105] The Godfearer renounced all forms of idolatry and embraced the higher moral principles that characterised Judaism. Considered 'associate members', they enjoyed fewer privileges than ethnic Jews.[106]

Where did the Godfearers stand with God?

---

[103] Called a גֵּר צַדִּיק (*ger tsaddiq*) in Hebrew, meaning a 'righteous stranger'. These enjoyed equal status with ethnic Jews. This tradition may have morphed into the modern concept of 'righteous gentiles' – those who risked their own lives to protect Jews, like Oskar Schindler.

[104] From the Greek version of Psalm 115:11 (Psalm 113:19 in the Septuagint) οἱ φοβούμενοι τὸν κύριον ['those who fear the Lord'].

[105] Hebrew: גֵּר וְתוֹשָׁב (*ger toshav*). The term comes from the Tanakh, for example, Leviticus 25:3

> *'If one of your brethren becomes poor ... you shall help him, like a stranger [Hebrew: ger] or a sojourner [Hebrew: toshav], that he may live with you.*

[106] For example, Godfearers were not permitted within the Jewish section of the Temple (along with ritually 'unclean' Jews).

The Mishnah records Jewish belief in the universal salvation of all Jews, which was inclusive of gentile proselytes:

> All Israel have a portion in the world to come, for it says, "Your people, all of them righteous, shall possess the land for ever; They are the shoot that I planted, my handiwork in which I glory" (Isaiah 60:21).[107]

Another ancient extrabiblical source document is called the *Tosefta,*[108] and contains explanations for difficult Mishnah texts and comments from the sages of the first two centuries CE.[109] Regarding the Mishnah quote above, Rabbi Eliezer is recorded as stating the outcome for Gentiles, including Godfearers:

> None of the gentiles has a portion in the world to come, as it is said, "The wicked shall return to Sheol, all the gentiles who forget God" (Ps. 9:17).

Other opinions are listed, and there is no evidence that a majority of Jews held to Eliezer's view. Nonetheless, it seems there were some who resisted the idea of Godfearers 'having an equal chance' for salvation.

With that in mind, let's now investigate the historical events that conspired to drive a wedge between Jewish and gentile worshippers of the God of Israel.

---

[107] m.*Sanhedrin*.10:1.

[108] Meaning 'addition' – it contains explanations for difficult Mishnah texts.

[109] Known as the period of the *Tannaim,* who were the sages that recorded the Mishnah.

Gentile Inclusion in The Way

Chapter ten of the Book of Acts[110] in the Apostolic Writings narrates the reluctant visit by the apostle *Shimon/Simon* (aka *Kepha*),[111] to a Roman Legionnaire and Godfearer named Cornelius. He was a Centurion within the Italian Cohort,[112] residing in Joppa.[113] Simon's reluctance to visit Cornelius was overcome by a vision, ***incorrectly*** interpreted by Christians to say that the laws of *kashrut*[114] had been abolished. According to Simon himself, through the vision, God revealed to him that gentiles were neither 'common nor unclean'.[115] Cornelius and his household became the first gentile adherents to 'The Way'. This was probably around 42 CE.

The previous chapter of Acts records the dramatic change of heart experienced by the Pharisee from Tarsus named

---

[110] The fifth (narrative) book in the Apostolic Writings. It's full name is the 'Acts of the Apostles', and describes how they went about Judea and the diaspora spreading their message, following the death of Yeshua.

[111] Commonly referred to as 'Simon-Peter' or simply 'Peter'. Yeshua renamed Shimon 'Kepha' [Hebrew: כֵּיפָא meaning 'stone'], but in the Greek text it a appears as *Petros* – hence 'Peter'.

[112] In Greek: σπείρης τῆς καλουμένης Ἰταλικῆς ['the cohort that's called 'Italian']. A Roman Legions (around 5000 men) was divided into ten cohorts of about 480 troops. *Cohorts* were made up of six *Centuria* (80 soldiers), each commanded by a *Centurion*. In the culture of his day, if Cornelius underwent a full conversion to Judaism he would have likely been discharged from the Army.

"Hmmm…do you find that *funny* Centurion?"

[113] Modern Jaffa. The location is also mentioned in the Tanakh as יָפוֹ (*yapho*) in Jonah 1:3; 2 Chronicles 2:16

[114] That is, the dietary restrictions in Torah: no pork, no shellfish, no rock badgers etc. See Leviticus 11 or Deuteronomy 14 for more specific information.

[115] Acts 10:28; cp. 11:9,18.

Sha'ul/Saul/Paulos/Paul. [116] He was to become the Apostle to the Gentiles, having a successful ministry among (primarily) the Godfearers in the synagogues of the diaspora, preaching a message of Jewish–Gentile equality in Yeshua's sect. He did not win too many popularity contests among his Jewish brethren with this missive, but he was a bit of a hit with the Gentile Godfearers, as you can imagine.

As the number of Gentiles within the sect grew, so did dissension within the group as to the status of these Godfearers. There was considerable pressure from the Jerusalem Jews, who insisting that the Gentiles needed to undergo a full proselyte conversion. Paul and the members in the diaspora did not subscribe to that proposition. A council assembled in Jerusalem around 48 CE to resolve the issue. After some debate, the Jerusalem leader of the sect, James[117] (Yeshua's brother) gave his decision that Gentile Godfearers could be admitted without conversion, but their minimum standard of conduct was to be in accord with other Godfearers in the mainstream synagogues:[118]

> *...[Gentiles are] to abstain from things polluted by idols, from sexual immorality, from things strangled, and from blood[shed].[119]*

An aspect of Gentile acceptance commonly **overlooked** by Christian expositors is that they were expected to grow in

---

[116] i.e. Saul, who was also known by his Greek name: *Paulos* i.e. 'Paul'.

[117] As we saw in the previous chapter his real name was Ya'akov (Jacob).

[118] These four principles are based on the seven commandments known as the 'Noachide Laws' – more on this later.

[119] Acts 15:20.

Torah obedience as their understanding increased, as James explained in the very next verse:

> *For Moses has had throughout many generations those who preach him in every city, being read in the synagogues every Sabbath.*[120]

Our previous diagram must now be altered to reflect Gentile acceptance in The Way.

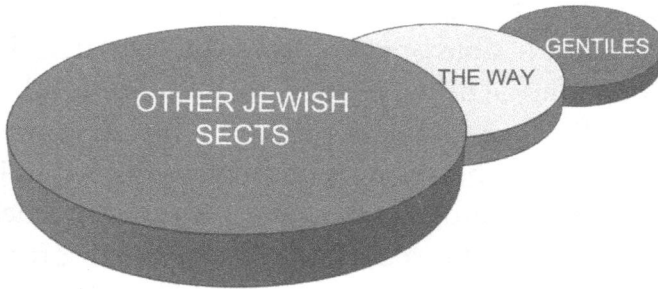

The First Jewish-Roman War

The first century Jewish historian Flavius Josephus records that the catalyst for the first Jewish-Roman war took place in Caesarea in 66 CE:

> [O]n the seventh day of the week, when the Jews were crowding apace to their synagogue, a certain man of Caesarea, of a seditious temper, got an earthen vessel, and set it with the bottom upward, at the entrance of that synagogue, and sacrificed birds.[121]

---

[120] Acts 15:20–21.

[121] Josephus, *War of the Jews*, II.14.5.

A complaint to the Roman Procurator, Gessius Florus, resulted in reprisal action against the plaintiffs(!) and the removal of Jewish silver and gold from the Temple treasury.[122] This inflamed Jewish-Gentile tensions to the point that the Roman fortress at Masada was successfully attacked and the Jewish High Priest ended the daily sacrifices offered on behalf of the emperor,[123] while both Gentile and Jewish sympathisers were killed by the growing band of Jewish rebels. The Legate of Syria, Cestius Gallus, sent a legion of troops to quell the uprising. They were defeated by the Jewish rebels at Bethoron.

Not surprisingly, Rome determined to crush the rebellion and General Titus was despatched to Judea accompanied by

...two legions with eight divisions of cavalry and ten cohorts.[124]

The early church historian Eusebius records that the Jewish followers of Yeshua in Jerusalem[125] escaped the Roman siege, having already fled to Pella,[126] east of the Jordan River.[127]

---

[122] Their plunder is estimated to be equivalent in today's terms to half a million US dollars.

[123] Those who failed to worship any Roman gods (including the emperor) were considered Atheists, a potentially capital crime (today, it's quite hip to be an atheist; then it was a death sentence. Ahh, those were the good old days!). In an agreement between Rome and the Jews, a daily sacrifice was offered in the Jewish temple, not *to* the emperor, but *on his behalf*. Accordingly, Judaism was granted legal status as a religion.

[124] Suetonius, *The Lives of the Twelve Caesars,* http://history-world.org/suetonius.pdf.

[125] The Apostolic Writings claim there were a vast number living in Jerusalem (Acts 21:17–20).

[126] In the Decapolis, not the Pella in modern Greece.

[127] Eusebius, *Church History,* III.5.3.

That being the case, the largest collection of ethnic Jewish followers of Yeshua in existence at the time were removed from their Gentile counterparts and mainstream Jewish brethren.

Fiscus Judaicus

A significant backlash against Jewry took place following the first Roman-Jewish War. Part of the Roman reprisal for the Jewish rebellion was the *Fiscus Judaicus,* a special poll tax imposed on all Jews aged three and upwards.[128] For the average Jewish household, the annual tax was the equivalent to 22 days wages.[129]

By the time Domitian was emperor, no official method was in place for properly deciding an individual's 'Jewishness' and liability to pay the tax. One of its unintended consequences was to force communities to define themselves as either Jewish or non-Jewish.[130] Under Domitian's successor, Nerva, the criterion for being subject to the tax was based, not on ethnicity, but on religious practice, especially Sabbath observance. Gentile followers of Yeshua began to argue that the actual day of the week in which one enjoyed a period of

---

[128] e.g. Martin Goodman, *Diaspora Reactions to the Destruction of the Temple,* in Dunn, James D.G. (ed.), *Jews and Christians: The Parting of the Ways AD 70 to 135,* (Eerdmans: Grand Rapids 1999), 30. The Torah prescribed a yearly half-shekel tax incumbent on all Jews over the age of twenty (Exodus 30:12-14). Jewish law allowed that it need not be paid if the Temple ever ceased to exist (m.*Shekalim*.8:8). Following the destruction of the Temple in 70 CE, Vespasian diverted the tax to the Temple of Jupiter Capitolinus at Rome, a huge affront to Jewish religious feelings.

[129] Christopher O'Quin, *The Growing Split Between Synagogue and Church in the First Century,* www.torahresource.com/English Articles/ Fiscus%20Judaicus.pdf (accessed 03 June 2023).

[130] *Ibid.*

rest was not particularly important and began to distance themselves from Jewish followers to avoid the tax. By then, most Jewish followers of Yeshua were already geographically separated from their mainstream ethnic brethren.

The three groups now had little or no overlap, with Gentile followers of Yeshua by now numerically greater than their Jewish counterparts, represented in the figure below.

MAINSTREAM JUDAISM

GENTILES OF THE WAY

JEWS OF THE WAY

The Council of Yavneh

When the city of Jerusalem came under Roman retribution, a number of Jews escaped including a Pharisee named Yochanan ben Zakkai. He was smuggled out of the city in a coffin to negotiate with the military commander Titus (aka Vespasian), whom he prophesied would become the emperor. Following the meeting Vespasian granted ben Zakkai permission to start a yeshiva[131] in Yavneh.[132] This school eventually took over the powers of the Great Sanhedrin, the legislative assembly that met most days in Jerusalem while the temple had stood.

---

[131] An institute of higher Jewish learning.

[132] Also known as 'Jamnia', it is situated in modern Israel.

Around 90 CE the Council of Yavneh was set up to examine the challenges facing those Jews who survived Titus' campaign, and especially how to continue in Judaism without a temple and priesthood as the locus for their worship. One of the outcomes was a stricter definition of who was, and who was not, Jewish. This was reflected in the newly introduced category in Judaism of *minim,* [133] This distinction found its way into the *Amidah,* [134] part of Jewish liturgy, following the Yavneh Council.

The Amidah has been repeated two or three times daily by religious Jews from antiquity to the present era. Following the Council of Yavneh, a nineteenth benediction (technically, a 'malediction') was added, called the *Birkat ha'Minim,* which petitions God to act against the heretics. [135]

Any covert followers of Yeshua would have been unlikely to pronounce a curse upon themselves. From the end of the first century, monotheism began to coalesce into two structurally and theologically separate religious camps: Gentile 'Christianity', as it had become known and what we'll call 'Post-Yavneh' or Rabbinic Judaism. Jewish followers of Yeshua became increasingly marginalised by both of the other religious entities.

---

[133] Literally [different] 'species' or 'group' and, by inference, 'heretics'.

[134] It is also known as the Sh'moneh Esreh (Hebrew for 'eighteen') because it consists of eighteen benedictions. The benedictions are recited while standing – the word Amidah comes from the Hebrew word עָמַד (amad) meaning 'to stand'.

[135] It was added as the twelfth benediction, so now there's nineteen in total. An English translation of the *Birkat ha'Minim* is:

As for heretics may there be no hope; may all the evil be instantly destroyed, and all Your enemies be cut down swiftly; as for the evil ones, uproot and break and destroy and humble them soon in our days. Blessed are you, LORD, who breaks down enemies and humbles the proud.

The illustration below shows the three distinct monotheistic religions by the early second century CE.

The Second Jewish Revolt

Within sixty years of the defeat by Rome, Jewish discontent at submission to the Roman yoke rose to the surface again. In 114 CE the Emperor Trajan conducted a successful military campaign against the Persian armies which included resident Jews who fought alongside their hosts. The victors turned their anger towards Jews throughout the Empire in a series of harsh measures which encouraged the Alexandrians to massacre the Jews in Egypt and destroy their synagogues.

The next emperor, Hadrian, initially took a conciliatory stance with the Jews even promising them that he would allow the rebuilding of the Temple, if they would give him their loyalty and support. Hadrian reneged on his promise (imagine that!), laying instead the foundation for a temple to the god Jupiter on the Temple Mount. The desire for rebellion intensified into open outrage.[136]

---

[136] Cassius Dio, Roman History LXIX.12. http://penelope.uchicago.edu/Thayer /E/Roman/Texts/Cassius _Dio/69*.html#12 (accessed 01 August 2023).

One of the most respected sages in Jerusalem at the time, Rabbi Akiva ben Yoseph,[137] heard of a courageous man of great religious fervour who was organising a guerrilla force to overthrow the Roman oppressors. The man's name was Shimon bar Kozeva. Akiva renamed him *Shimon bar Kokhva*,[138] and endorsed his claim to be the Messiah. Those Jews who were followers of Yeshua (predictably) refused to acknowledge him as such.[139]

The rebel forces under bar Kokhva enjoyed initial success even minting coins (c. 133 CE) for their new free state, but their faith proved misplaced:

> Bar Kokhva and his forces eventually made their last stand against the Romans... in the year 135 CE, and there Bar Kokhva met his death... Jews were not permitted to enter [Jerusalem]... and a temple to Jupiter... [was] built on the old temple site.[140]

Any vestige of relationship between mainstream Judaism and Jewish followers of Yeshua was irrevocably destroyed at this point. The Yeshua group in Jerusalem underwent significant leadership changes after the failed bar Kokhva uprising. The fourth century CE church historian Eusebius of Caesarea recorded that there had been fifteen Jewish leaders in

---

[137] It's claimed that he lived to the age of 120 – quite an achievement at any time in antediluvian history.

[138] 'bar Kokhva' (also spelled 'Kochba') means 'son of a star' – a reference to the messianic prophecy in Numbers 24:17.

[139] Instead, they said, "He's just a naughty boy!"

[140] James C. VanderKam, *An Introduction to Early Judaism*, (Grand Rapids: Eerdmans 2001), 49.

Jerusalem from the time of *Ya'akov ha Tsaddiq*,[141] and the next fifteen were all Gentiles. The Way had become the gentile institution we know today as the Christian Church.

And what of the Jewish followers of Yeshua? The community in Pella referred to themselves as the *Ebionites*.[142] Despised by both mainstream Jews and the Gentile Christian Church (which had now become an arm of the Roman Empire), they died out by the fifth century, leaving the two faiths we have today, the latter having vastly outgrown its Jewish origins.

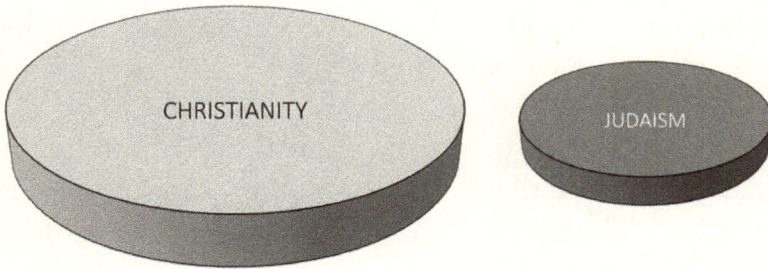

CHRISTIANITY

JUDAISM

Under the first century leadership of James, Gentiles were allowed entry into 'The Way' without proselyte conversion. Sadly, the Christian Church did not offer the same courtesy to Jews. Jews who converted to Christianity – which was originally an exclusively Jewish sect – had to renounce all rituals and practices of Jewish origin – the very things that Yeshua would have enjoyed and endorsed.

Worse, the official Roman Church became increasingly antisemitic with every passing century, embarking on periodic

---

[141] 'James the Just'. As mentioned previously, he was one of Yeshua's four brothers.

[142] From the Hebrew word: אֶבְיוֹנִים (*Evionim*), meaning 'poor ones'.

waves of horrific persecution of Jews – without whom, they would have never been introduced to the one true God in the first place.

What's the Bottom Line?

A series of historical events severed the already tenuous link between mainstream Jews and Jewish followers of Yeshua. Within about 100 years of the death of Yeshua, the Jewish sect called 'The Way' had become an exclusively gentile faith and began to deny the Jewish aspects of their religion. The dwindling number of Jewish followers of Yeshua, marginalised by both groups, eventually died out.

By the fourth century, Christianity, a gentile religion, had become an arm of the Roman Empire, and a champion of antisemitism. The message the first Jewish followers of Yeshua had proclaimed degenerated into a syncretistic blending of scripture with Hellenistic philosophy and pagan religious practices.

That's an outline of how we got from there to here. Now comes the tricky bit – hunting down and killing or subduing our three resident elephants.

Stick with me.

Please.

Part Two:
Mini-Jumbo

Photo: Rob Hampson - Upsplash

In the introduction, I said that this composite elephant consists of unnecessary areas of discord between Jews and Christians that have resulted from misunderstanding.

Although there are many such issues, this section will examine three common misconceptions, primarily arising from Christianity's failure to view the Apostolic Writings through the prism of Second Temple Judaism.

First up, in chapter two, I hope to demonstrate that Torah is eternal and unchanging. In the third chapter, I'll consider those texts in the Tanakh and Apostolic Writings that Christians have used to affirm belief in eternal damnation for the lost[143] and, in chapter four I hope to refute the Jewish idea that Paul ruined an otherwise reasonable Jewish sect.

But, I hear you say, "What happened to chapter one?"

Ah... well, it's like this, you see... there's some more foundational stuff we need to talk about before proceeding into the main objectives of this section of the book.

Sorry 'bout that.

But to fully grasp the topics of this section I need my readers (especially those of the Christian persuasion) to thoroughly understand the significance of God's covenants with human beings.

We already have sufficient ado, so without any further requirement for the stuff...

---

[143] Popular Christianity teaches that the lost includes anybody who rejects the Lordship of Yeshua, even if they've never heard of him.

Chapter One:
What's a Covenant?

To begin with it's not a tiny insect that just happens to belong to a witches' circle. As I've no doubt my readers are aware, it is a legally (and morally) binding agreement – like a treaty or contract. Here's my take on it in a less prosaic form:

In days of old, when kings were bold and democracies weren't invented, there were different kinds of covenants that sometimes folk resented.[144]

There were two main types of covenants in the ancient Near East, upon which I shall now wax elephant.[145]

The Royal Grant

A Royal Grant covenant was when a powerful ruler gave a subordinate leader a gift, typically of land and sovereignty, as a reward with, more or less, no strings attached. Beautiful Blenheim Palace in England sits on 2000 spectacular acres that were originally given as a royal grant to the Duke of Marlborough and his descendants following his victory at the Battle of Blenheim in 1704.

---

[144] Yes, you're right. I shouldn't give up my day job in pursuit of the poet laureate's title.

[145] Sorry about that I should have said 'eloquent' – I've obviously got the silly creatures on my mind.

There are biblical examples of the royal grant covenant. For example, God's promises to Abram in Genesis chapter twelve – repeated in other texts within the book of Genesis – were unconditional.[146]

The Suzerain-Vassal Covenant

In this agreement a powerful ruler, the Suzerain, made a conditional covenant with a lesser person, the Vassal. Following the conquest of a nation, it was not uncommon for the victorious suzerain to leave the vanquished king as sovereign over his own nation, as long as he kept the rules imposed by the suzerain. Typically, these would include the vassal's oath of fealty, the payment of taxes and the implementation of policies in accordance with the suzerain's interests.

The covenant that God made with the newly formed Hebrew nation at Mount Sinai was a suzerain-vassal covenant. God promised manifold blessings to the descendants of the twelve tribes of Israel. In return, they were to be obedient to the statutes of Torah. Failure to do so would result in the forfeit of God's promised blessings.[147]

How About the Rest of Us?

Every person on planet Earth is in a covenant relationship with God, whether they know it or not. Most of mankind is

---

[146] Please note, dear Christians that God's unconditional grant included the land from the River of Egypt to the Euphrates (Genesis 15:18). I beseech you not to fall for any claims to the contrary by the Palestinian people (so-called).

[147] Deuteronomy 28:1-68.

bound by the Noachide Covenant – the one that God made with the descendants of Noah, which embraces almost everyone.[148]

Believe it or not, few Christians consider the Noachide Covenant to be relevant today, assuming it has been rescinded. Allow me to quote the pertinent text from Genesis to which encapsulates the main tenets of mankind's responsibilities under the terms of the agreement:

> *Whoever sheds man's blood, by man his blood shall be shed; for in the image of God He made man. And as for you, be fruitful and multiply; bring forth abundantly in the earth and multiply in it. By man his blood shall be shed; for in the image of God He made man.*[149]

Judaism explored this covenant deducing seven Noachide laws, applicable to all men. One of them was a positive injunction – that all human societies were to establish a judicial system. The other six are prohibitions. They forbid idolatry, blasphemy, murder, sexual immorality, theft and eating flesh torn from a living animal.

For my Christian readers who may be inclined to dismiss the Noachide Covenant as a mere construct of Judaism, these seven commandments can be further reduced to four basic principles. The Apostolic Writings prove that these principles were accepted by the Jewish leaders of the burgeoning sect (which would eventually morph into Christianity) as binding

---

[148] I say 'just about' because some are held to a higher standard through a different covenant.

[149] Genesis 9:6-7. Verse 8 confirms that this covenant is with all the descendants of Noah and, indeed, all the animals as well.

on Gentiles. Assuming a judicial system is in place, the guidance is that Gentiles are to refrain from murder, idolatry, sexual immorality, and consuming live animals. Leaders of the followers of Yeshua convened a council in Jerusalem around 48 CE to decide whether those gentiles embracing their sect had to undergo a full conversion to Judaism. Their decision was that they did not have to do so. Instead, they had to keep the four Noachide principles as a bare minimum for membership.[150]

So, What's the Bottom Line?

The principles of the covenant that God made with the descendants of Noah (that's everybody born since the flood) are the minimum standard to which all mankind is held accountable.

I say 'minimum standard' because God has made special covenants with both individuals[151] and groups of people. These agreements, such as the covenant of Torah, obligate those under its authority to a higher standard of conduct (with greater promises from God in return).

Non-Jews are born under the Noachide laws; Jews are born under the Torah covenant.

---

[150] Acts 15:19-20. Note that 'blood' in v.20 refers to 'bloodshed'. As mentioned in the introduction to this book, in the very next breath (v.21) Yeshua's brother James gives the reason for such a low benchmark:

For Moses has had throughout many generations those who preach him in every city, being read in the synagogues every Sabbath.

James anticipated that Gentile members in their sect would grow in Torah obedience as time went on.

[151] e.g., Abraham and David.

What about the promised New Covenant?

We'll get to that in the fulness of time...

Chapter Two:
Bye Bye Torah?

And the statutes, the ordinances, the law, and the commandment which He wrote for you, you shall be careful to observe forever...[152]

The purpose of this section is to refute the notion held by some (not all) Christians that the Torah was but an interim measure, expressing God's will for his people – but only for a season. A further development of this idea, opined sometimes in Evangelical circles, is that God gave Torah to Israel for the express purpose of proving to them that it was impossible to keep(!).

Why would God foist a code of conduct upon his chosen people that was totally beyond their ability? How could David extol the virtues of Torah in the longest psalm in the Tanakh[153] if it were an unbearable imposition? The words of Moses contradict this nonsensical hypothesis:

For this commandment which I command you today is not too mysterious for you, nor is it far off. It is not in heaven, that you should say, 'Who will ascend into heaven for us and bring it to us, that we may hear it and do it?' Nor is it

---

[152] 2 Kings 17:37a. The psalmist expresses the same fact in different words:

> ...*All [God's] precepts are sure. they stand fast forever and ever...* (Psalm 117:.7b-8a).

[153] Psalm 119 has 176 verses. Psalm 78 is second longest with 72 verses.

beyond the sea, that you should say, 'Who will go over the sea for us and bring it to us, that we may hear it and do it?' [154]

If Torah-observance was beyond human ability, why are our Western democracies, with their Judeo-Christian roots, founded on its principles? Simply put, Torah defines absolute standards of right and wrong from God's perspective.[155]

The confusion arises partly from a Christian assumption that Torah-compliance means the same thing as being 'perfect' or 'sinless'. They forget that there were provisions for sin under the Torah itself.[156] But the main problem is the misguided teaching (promoted by some) that Yeshua abolished Torah.[157]

Have a think about that...

These folks maintain that Yeshua is the Messiah of Israel who chose to overturn the very foundation of Israel's existence. If Yeshua taught anyone that Torah was not to be observant, that was tantamount to telling his disciples to follow a different god. In other words, he was a false prophet and therefore deserving of death under the Torah itself.[158]

---

[154] Deuteronomy 30:11-13.

[155] Obviously, we're all grown up now. That's why our societies are rejecting more and more of God's holy commandments as time goes on.

[156] Leviticus chapters four and five detail the requirements for the sin and trespass offerings and all of Israel's transgressions were forgiven annually at Yom Kippur for those who turned back to God (e.g., Leviticus 16:21ff).

[157] To be fair, this viewpoint is held by a small minority of Christians.

[158] Deuteronomy 13:4-5.

But wait, there's more…

Yeshua plainly insisted that his mission had nothing to do with the abolition of Torah:

Do not think that I came to destroy the Law or the Prophets. I did not come to destroy but to fulfil. For assuredly, I say to you, till heaven and earth pass away, one jot or one tittle [159] *will by no means pass from the law till all is fulfilled.* [160]

Last time I looked, both heaven and earth were still here. Just in case his audience didn't get it, Yeshua continued:

Whoever therefore breaks one of the least of these commandments, and teaches men so, shall be called least in the kingdom of heaven; but whoever does and teaches them, he shall be called great in the kingdom of heaven. [161]

There's a degree of irony in this perspective. Christians who hold this opinion inevitably point to the writings of Sha'ul of Tarsus[162] to prove their argument. They are unaware this self-

---

[159] 'Jot and tittle' comes from ἰῶτα… κεραία *(iota… keraia).* But this is an attempt to translate his original Hebrew (or Aramaic) into Greek. His original words were highly likely to have been: קוֹצוֹ שֶׁל יוֹד *(qotzo shel yod)* – or its Aramaic equivalent – which means, 'the tiniest mark on the smallest letter'.

[160] Matthew 5:17-19.

[161] Matthew 5:20. By the way, dear Christians, 'kingdom of heaven' doesn't mean 'heaven'. It means the earthly kingdom wherein Messiah rules from David's throne in Jerusalem. 'Heaven' is a circumlocution for 'God' out of sensitivity to Matthew's Jewish readers.

[162] Saul of Tarsus was a Pharisee, advanced beyond his years in Judaism. He is better known by his Greek name Paulos i.e., Paul as we refer to him elsewhere.

same Sha'ul/Paul declared that he was Torah-observant in the Apostolic Writings:

> *...concerning the righteousness which is in the law, [I was] blameless.*[163]

How is this misconception possible? Well, we'll get to that in chapter four, when we look more closely at this much-misunderstood Apostle. For now, though, suffice to say that the earliest Gentile adherents of the Christian religion decided that Torah was still very much a valid code and that they would do well to walk according to its precepts.

The earliest record we have outside the Apostolic Writings is found in a document called the *Didache*.[164] Regarding Torah observance, the guidance given to gentile Christians is as follows:

> *...if you are able to bear the entire [torah], you will be perfect; but if you are not able to do this, do what you are able. And concerning food, bear what you are able; but against that which is sacrificed to idols be exceedingly careful...*[165]

This position is compatible with the Apostolic Writings themselves.

---

[163] Philippians 3:6b. See also Acts: 25:8; 26:5.

[164] Its full title is διδαχή κυρίου διὰ τῶν δώδεκα ἀποστόλων τοῖς ἔθνεσιν (*didache kuriou dia ton dodeka apostolon tois ethnesin*), meaning: *The Lord's Teaching Through the Twelve Apostles to the Gentiles*. It was written as a manual for gentile Christians by an unknown author in the late first century CE.

[165] Didache 6:1b-3a.

Recall that the **minimum standard** for gentile acceptance into the early Jewish sect of *The Way* was compliance with the Noachide Laws. However, gentiles were encouraged to keep more than the minimum standard as noted in the decision of the Jerusalem Council. Gentiles attending those assemblies where Jewish members of *The Way* gathered, would become more familiar with Torah, over time and the clear inference is that they would become more observant as their knowledge grew.

What a shame that outlook didn't last.

So, What's the Bottom Line?

The bottom line is simply that Gentile followers of Yeshua are encouraged to keep as much Torah as they are able. How can Gentiles be considered 'holy' if their obedience is defined by a sliding scale between Noachide laws and Torah?

Very easily. The Apostle Paul explains in his letter to the assembly in Rome that Gentiles are sanctified (made holy) by the Jewish Torah-observing members of the sect.[166]

That's another little slice from the irony pie, isn't it?

---

[166] Romans 11:13-18. Paul uses the illustration of a lump of dough sanctifying the loaf and the root of a cultivated olive tree (Israel) supporting the wild branches that have been grafted-in (Gentiles).

Chapter Three:
Well, I'll be Damned!

In this chapter, I want to tackle the popular Christian notion that those who reject Yeshua will suffer the fires of eternal punishment. This belief had its origins in Hellenistic philosophy and is reinforced by certain texts in the Apostolic Writings, interpreted without applying the Hebraic contextual understanding of the day.

The Messianic Kingdom

The Tanakh has many passages describing what it will be like when Messiah comes to rule over a restored earth from David's throne in Jerusalem.[167] The Apostolic Writings teach the same thing. Yeshua plainly believed that he was this Messiah and declared that, in the Messianic Kingdom, he would appoint his twelve closest followers as governors over Israel:

So Jesus said to them, "Assuredly I say to you, that in the regeneration, when the Son of Man sits on the throne of His glory, you who have followed Me will also sit on twelve thrones, judging the twelve tribes of Israel."[168]

---

[167] Isaiah 65:17–25, for example.

[168] Matthew 19:28.

My Jewish readers will be keen to point out that Yeshua clearly didn't fulfil this pledge. Regardless, the first Christians believed that Yeshua rose from the dead and would return in the future to rule from Jerusalem as he promised.

The Tanakh reveals that, when Messiah comes, God will overthrow all the kingdoms of this world and set up his own kingdom which cannot be dislodged. The Babylonian ruler, Nebuchadnezzar, had a disturbing dream about a great statue.[169] Daniel explained that it represented various empires that would, someday, succumb to the kingdom of God:

> *And in the days of these kings the God of heaven will set up a kingdom which shall never be destroyed; and the kingdom shall not be left to other people; it shall break in pieces and consume all these kingdoms, and it shall stand forever. Inasmuch as you saw that the stone was cut out of the mountain without hands, and that it broke in pieces the iron, the bronze, the clay, the silver, and the gold—the great God has made known to the king what will come to pass after this. The dream is certain, and its interpretation is sure.* [170]

The early Christians clung to this prophetic text during the waves of persecution inflicted on them by various Roman Emperors until the end of the third century CE. But with the supposed conversion of the Emperor Constantine I in 312 CE, it wasn't long before Christianity was declared official religion of Rome and the church devolved into an organ of the state.

---

[169] Daniel 2:31–45.

[170] Daniel 2:44–45.

Now that the mighty Roman Empire was a 'Christian' kingdom, the overthrow of earthly kingdoms at Messiah's coming could no longer be taken literally. Thus, the Messianic Kingdom was spiritualised to mean something other than a literal earthly realm. The consensus among church historians is that belief in an earthly kingdom was condemned at the Council of Ephesus in 431 CE.

The Implications of an Earthly Kingdom

The Apostolic Writings assert that the earthly kingdom of Messiah is of a finite duration.[171] Moreover, only the righteous will enjoy life in the messianic kingdom which precedes the final judgment. If they have already died, they will be resurrected to enjoy life in messianic age.

Whither the wicked?

Those who die prior to the Messiah's coming are consigned to a place of punishment called Gehinnom.[172] In the Tanakh the place of the dead is referred to as *Sheol*. Unfortunately, some English bibles translate this word as 'hell' with all the

---

[171] The book of Revelation is an apocalyptic writing replete with symbolism. However, if the duration is meant to be taken literally, the earthly kingdom will stand for a thousand years (Revelation 20:1-6), to be followed by the final judgment of the dead and the eternal state, whatever that may be.

[172] This is from the Hebrew גֵּיא־הִנֹּם , meaning the 'Valley of Hinnom'. This is a geographical location to the south and southwest of Jerusalem which, in the Second Temple era, was the community rubbish dump. Here, refuse and animal corpses were burned for disposal. As a smelly, unpleasant place, it became a metaphor for the place of punishment for the wicked dead. Its Aramaic equivalent is *gehanna,* which is transliterated in the Greek of the Apostolic Writings as γέεννα (ge'enna).

Dante-esque images that conjures. For instance, David refers to Sheol in his psalm extolling the omnipresence of God:

> *If I ascend into heaven, You are there; if I make my bed in hell,* [173] *behold, You are there.* [174]

By the Second Temple era, Jewish writings reveal that Sheol was divided into two major sections: one for the righteous dead and the other for the wicked. The latter section, Gehinnom, was also known as 'Torments'. The righteous dead were accommodated in the section which is known by names attempting to describe it. It's called Paradise,[175] or Abraham's lap, [176] or *Gan-Eden*, which is Hebrew for the Garden of Eden.[177]

Whichever side the souls of the dead reside, they are awaiting physical and literal resurrection.

Now consider this excerpt from parable taught by Yeshua as recorded in Luke's narrative:

> *There was a certain rich man who was clothed in purple and fine linen and fared sumptuously every day. But there was a certain beggar named Lazarus, full of sores, who was laid at his gate, desiring to be fed with the crumbs which*

---

[173] Literally שְׁאוֹל (she'ol).

[174] Psalm 139:8.

[175] Pardes (פַּרְדֵּס) comes from Persian word meaning a beautiful garden. It is the mnemonic used to represent the four stages of Hebrew exposition, as we saw earlier on.

[176] To dine, reclining against Father Abraham was the highest honour that a Jew could receive in the afterlife.

[177] בַּן-עֵדֶן

fell from the rich man's table. Moreover the dogs came and licked his sores. So it was that the beggar died, and was carried by the angels to Abraham's bosom. The rich man also died and was buried. And being in torments in Hades, he lifted up his eyes and saw Abraham afar off, and Lazarus in his bosom. [178]

This parable is in keeping with Second Temple Jewish thought. The righteous Lazarus, who suffered in his earthly life and rewarded at death is taken to Abraham's bosom – the actual Greek word is κόλπος *(kolpos)* which describes the area from the waist to the shoulders. Lazarus is portrayed as reclining in Abraham's lap.

In contrast, the selfish rich man is transported at death to 'Torments[179] in Hades'. This is the unpleasant half of Sheol, since Hades (ᾅδης) is the Greek term (borrowed from Hellenism) used to translate Sheol in the Septuagint, the Greek translation of the Tanakh. Here's that verse from psalm 139, quoted earlier – this time from the Septuagint:

If I should go up to heaven, you are there. If I should go down to Hades, you are present. [180]

---

[178] Luke 16:19-23.

[179] The plural 'torments' correctly reflects the Greek βασάνοις *(basanois)*, the plural form of *basanos* (singular). Some English translations incorrectly render it in the singular as 'torment' reinforcing the Christian concept of Hell.

[180] Psalm 138:8 (LXX). There is sometimes a difference in chapter numbers between the Masoretic Text and the Septuagint. The word Hades appears in the second last word of the Greek text:

ἐὰν ἀναβῶ εἰς τὸν οὐρανόν, σὺ εἶ ἐκεῖ, ἐὰν καταβῶ εἰς τὸν ᾅδην, πάρει.

If anybody is wondering why Hades appears as ᾅδην (had<u>e</u>n) rather than ᾅδης (hades) as I stated in the body of my text – the former is simply the noun in the accusative

How Long, O Lord?

According to the Mishnah, the longest a wicked soul can remain in Gehinnom is twelve months.[181] Although the Talmud indicates that the very wicked may remain there for "generations and generations."[182] The same Talmudic tractate declares that although Gehinnom itself may be consumed, the wicked therein will not be:

Gehenna will be consumed [by fire], but they will not be consumed.[183]

The Apostolic Writings confirm the consumption by fire of Gehinnom/Hades, albeit in the apocalyptic style of Revelation:

Then Death and Hades were cast into the lake of fire.[184]

This statement occurs in the same chapter which mentions, no less than six times, the 1000-year duration of the earthly messianic kingdom. It sets the destruction of Gehinnom at the conclusion of the kingdom age.

What are we to make of this?

---

case. If you don't know what I mean by that grammatical term, consider yourself truly blessed!

[181] m.Eduyyot.2:10. Offences serious enough to warrant this treatment are also listed in the passage.

[182] b.Rosh Hashanah.17a.

[183] *Ibid.*

[184] Revelation 20:14a.

Well, it seems that there is no contradiction between the Apostolic Writings and traditional Jewish beliefs. The wicked are consigned to Gehinnom for a finite period of time – perhaps generations and generations – and the irredeemably evil may be punished even beyond the destruction of Gehinnom itself. The verse in the Book of Revelation which follows the destruction of Gehinnom states that a final judgment will occur at the end of the messianic era, where the incorrigibly wicked will be:

> *...cast into the lake of fire.*[185]

Along with death and Gehinnom, Satan and the political and religious evil final empire (symbolised by the titles 'beast' and 'false prophet' respectively) will suffer the fate of the lake of fire where:

> *...they will be tormented day and night forever and ever.*[186]

There is no difference between ancient Jewish belief and those of the first Christians, notwithstanding two minor details: Judaism asserts that most people will not need to endure more than twelve months in Gehinnom;[187] the Apostolic Writings decline to address this timeframe. The Apostolic Writings declare that the final judgment occurs at the end of the messianic age which lasts for a thousand years. Ancient Jewish writings offer different durations for this age.[188]

---

[185] Revelation 20:15.

[186] Revelation 20:10b.

[187] This sentence is reduced to eleven months for Jewish folks.

[188] For example, the pseudepigraphal 4 Ezra (aka 2 Esdras) specifies a messianic age of 400 years (4 Ezra 7:26–29).

Where Have All the Good Guys Gone?

As noted above, Sheol/Hades has two sections: Gehinnom for the wicked and Paradise for the righteous, where both groups await their physical resurrection from the dead. The Greco-Roman world rejected the idea of literal resurrection in favour of an eternal disembodied state of some kind – just as many world religions do. According to the Apostolic Writings, Paul proclaimed the resurrection of the dead in Athens at the Areopagus on Mars Hill to mixed results from the Greek intelligentsia of the day: And when they heard of the resurrection of the dead, some mocked, while others said, "We will hear you again on this matter." [189]

Although resurrection features prominently in all the historic creeds of the Christian Church, the Hellenistic attitude still prevails to a large degree. Somehow, along the way, the goal of a Christian became to 'go to heaven' when they die, spending eternity in a non-corporeal existence.

The Christian religion is founded on the belief that Yeshua was literally and physically resurrected from the grave around two thousand years ago. If nothing else, that should provide Christians with a hope for their own future resurrection as per his example. Not only that, but the Apostolic Writings also declare that he will return as Messiah to his last known address, the city of Jerusalem. [190]

Suppose for a moment that that's true. The next question, if there is no resurrection of the dead, would have to be:

---

[189] Acts 17:32.

[190] To be geographically precise, the Mount of Olives (Acts 1:1-11).

Why?

Why come back to this humble planet if everybody who ever lived is spending all of forever in heaven or hell? It just doesn't make sense.

But wait, there's more…

Most Christians believe that between death and resurrection, Yeshua visited Sheol and **rescued** all the faithful folks (e.g., Abraham, Moses, David etc.) and whisked them away to heaven(!). This idea is based on one obscure text in the Apostolic Writings,[191] taken out of context and horribly misinterpreted. Especially when two texts in the Apostolic Writings confirm the abode of the righteous dead as being Paradise.

The first example is a record of the words of Yeshua to a repentant criminal being crucified alongside him:

> *And Jesus said to him, "Assuredly, I say to you, today you will be with me in Paradise."* [192]

To the Christian Church, that statement presented no problem. They simply assumed that Paradise was just a synonym for Heaven.

What's wrong with that assumption?

---

[191] Ephesians 4:8. In its context, it's a midrash on Psalm 68:18 to affirming the different spiritual gifts available to people.

[192] Luke 23:43.

What's wrong with it, is that the Gospel of John records an encounter in the cemetery between Yeshua, freshly risen from the dead, and one of his female followers, Miriam from Magdala.[193] His words to her confirm that, between death and resurrection, his temporary abode was not heaven:

Jesus said to her, "Do not cling to me, for I have not yet ascended to my Father; but go to my brethren and say to them, 'I am ascending to my Father and your Father, and to my God and your God.'" [194]

Rather, as he declared to the repentant criminal, he had been in Paradise.

The second instance requires a little bit of background information. During the Second Temple period, a belief within Judaism arose in multiple 'heavens'.[195] Paradise is often said to be in the third heaven.[196]

The Apostle Paul describes a bizarre and (possibly) out-of-body experience in his second letter to the assembly at Corinth. Despite the third person language, he is actually referring to himself:

I know a man in Christ who fourteen years ago—whether in the body I do not know, or whether out of the body I do not know, God knows—such a one was caught up to

---

[193] Hebrew: מִרְיָם הַמַּגְדָּלִית Commonly known by her English name, Mary Magdalene.

[194] John 20:17. Given that God resides in Heaven e.g., Psalm 11:4.

[195] Usually seven e.g., b.*Chagigah.*12b; Apoc.Abr 19; Test.Levi 2:7-9; Asc. Isaih 10:17; 2 Enoch 8:1-6.

[196] 2 Enoch 8:5-6.

the third heaven. And I know such a man—whether in the body or out of the body I do not know, God knows—how he was caught up into Paradise and heard inexpressible words, which it is not lawful for a man to utter.[197]

In the above text, Paul confirms the location of Paradise as being in the 'third Heaven'.

So far there has been little variance between Second Temple Jewish thought and the Apostolic Writings. However, there is still another obstacle to investigate.

How Long is Forever?

I know, it sounds like a trick question. But, against the backdrop of eternity, is forever the same thing? I submit that 'forever' implies a duration, whereas eternity seems to describe a total absence of time, for time would surely be a meaningless concept in an eternal state?

Although, a cognate of a Modern Hebrew term meaning forever (in the sense of 'perpetuity'),[198] appears in the Tanakh on a number of occasions, more frequently in the Hebraic thought of biblical times, 'forever' was a contextual concept, more often translated by an expression meaning 'until the

---

[197] 2 Corinthians 12:2-4. In context, Paul is defending his ministry against so-called 'super apostles' [lit: 'over-great apostles' – Greek: ὑπερλίαν ἀποστόλων *(huperlian apostolon)*] who were beguiling the gullible with their tales of mystical experiences. In contrast to their arrogance, Paul uses the third person as seen in the next verse:

Of such a one I will boast; yet of myself I will not boast, except in my infirmities. (2 Corinthians 12:5).

[198] לָנֶצַח *(lanetzach)* e.g. *He will swallow up death* **forever**... *(Isaiah 25:8a).*

age'[199] or something similar. It can be compared to the notion of visibility, which varies according to specific environmental circumstances, such as time of day, weather conditions and elevation or altitude. A common enough English expression serves as a useful working definition of 'forever' from a biblical perspective. It is:

For the foreseeable future.

with emphasis on the term 'foreseeable' in regard to the context of its use.

Plainly, 'forever' from God's perspective is forever – since his 'visibility' of time is without end in either direction. By way of contrast, consider this text from the Torah, which prescribes the mandatory release of a slave[200] or bondservant after six years of service:

> *But if the servant plainly says, 'I love my master, my wife, and my children; I will not go out free,' then his master shall bring him to the judges. He shall also bring him to the door, or to the doorpost, and his master shall pierce his ear with an awl; and he shall serve him forever.*[201]

There are many examples of this usage of expressions translated 'forever' in our English bibles. In the above case, the term

---

[199] עַד־עוֹלָם *(ad-olam).* As an aside, the word 'olam' can also mean 'world' or 'universe' and appears in the start of many Hebrew blessings: "Blessed are You ,O Lord our God, King of the **universe**..."

[200] Biblical slavery was very different from its more modern counterpart. Except for prisoners-of-war, slavery was a voluntary option for an insolvent Jew. He would commit to six years servitude in return for board and keep and was often considered a member of the family.

[201] Exodus 21:5–6.

'forever' means 'for the term of his working life'. Contextually, that's as far as the slave and his owner could 'see'.

Forever and Ever?

Twenty-five times in the Tanakh we find the expression, 'forever and ever'. Surely this means for all eternity? Consider its usage below:

The LORD shall reign forever and ever.[202]

There can be no doubt that the Lord's reign is endless. Even the Hebrew text reads: לְעֹלָם וָעֶד *(l'olam va'ed)* – roughly 'to the age and more so'. Can we find this expression used in reference to an event of finite duration?

Sort of.

In Psalm 145 David combines the phrase with the finite term 'day' in this Hebrew parallelism:[203]

Every day I will bless You, and I will praise Your name forever and ever.[204]

---

[202] Exodus 15:18.

[203] A Hebrew parallelism is a poetic device whereby the same thing is expressed in two different ways, to aid memorisation. In Western cultures we use rhyme to achieve the same aim.

[204] Psalm 145:2.

And you're right, I am being unnecessarily pedantic. A similar example, using a different expression, [205] appears in the prophecies of Jeremiah:

> *if you do not oppress the stranger, the fatherless, and the widow, and do not shed innocent blood in this place, or walk after other gods to your hurt, then I will cause you to dwell in this place, in the land that I gave to your fathers forever and ever.*[206]

It is entirely possible that Israel will dwell in the Promised Land throughout eternity but, the probable meaning here is for the duration of the Messianic Age, as the Talmud affirms.[207]

From these few examples I propose that, in Hebraic thought, 'forever' is a flexible term dependent upon its context.

Eternal Life or Punishment?

Having determined that the Hebraic view of eternity is contextual, it is likely that the Jewish authors of the Apostolic Writings held to this view of forever in their writings. As it turns out, the Greek word for eternity allows this degree of flexibility. It is the word αἰώνιος *(aionios)* and its literal meaning is 'age-lasting' or 'for the duration of the age'.[208]

---

[205] עוֹלָם וְעַד־עוֹלָם *(olam v'ad olam)* – 'age and beyond the age'.

[206] Jeremiah 7:6-7, emphasis mine.

[207] b.*Sanhedrin*.99a states: 'All the prophets prophesied… only in respect of the Messianic era…'

[208] The root of the word is αἰών *(aion)* from which we get the English word aeon – a long period of time.

Consider the implications of a word which means for the duration of the age under consideration. Earlier in this chapter I stated that the first Christians believed that the Kingdom of God would follow this age, in which Messiah would rule on planet earth for centuries.

Beyond the Kingdom Age?

That's probably not something too many Second Temple Hebrewsmen gave thought to – it's more the type of question that a Greeksman would ask. However, the Gentile Christians of the first couple of centuries CE decided that the Messianic Age would be followed by an eternal state of some kind.

Here's the thing: if the Apostolic Writings refer to a period of time that lasts for 'an age' in the future, it is referring to the Kingdom of God. When the idea of an earthly kingdom was discarded by the Christian Church in the fifth century CE,[209] the age to come could only mean *eternity*.

To make that standpoint work, there could be no intermediate state for the dead, such as Sheol. Rather, there had to be eternal bliss in heaven (not on earth). The only available alternative became eternal damnation in the fires of hell.

---

[209] I should point at that a handful of Christians clung tenaciously to the earthly kingdom view over the centuries and that it made a significant comeback in the nineteenth century CE. At least among Evangelical Christianity, it is today the dominant opinion once more.

Consider the question that an expert in Torah[210] asked Yeshua:

And behold, a certain lawyer stood up and tested Him, saying, "Teacher, what shall I do to inherit eternal life?" [211]

Excursus

According to popular Christianity, the man was asking how to go to heaven forever. Accordingly, the response from Yeshua should have been:

"Ditch your obsession with that old law of Moses and put your faith in me."

We know that he was asking about entry into the Messianic Era. Yeshua, who some say abolished Torah, contradicts that false belief by the dialogue which follows:

He said to him, "What is written in the law? What is your reading of it?" So he answered and said, "'You shall love the LORD your God with all your heart, with all your soul, with all your strength, and with all your mind,' and 'your neighbor as yourself.'" [212]

Among the scholars of the day, it was commonplace to reduce the 613 mitzvot to a smaller summary, choosing those

---

[210] The English text translates the Greek word νομικός *(nomikos)* as 'lawyer'. His Jewish contemporaries would have described him as a בַּעַל תּוֹרָה (ba'al Torah), literally a 'Master of Torah'.

[211] Luke 10:25.

[212] Luke 10:26-27.

commandments that were all-embracing. This was Yeshua's opportunity to correct this man's mistaken belief in the centrality of Torah:

> *And He said to him, "You have answered rightly; do this and you will live."* [213]

Instead of reproving the scholar, Yeshua confirmed his Torah summary based on Deuteronomy 6:5 and Leviticus 19:18. But he could scarcely do otherwise, could he? In Jerusalem prior to his death, Yeshua was asked the same question as the one he had posed previously to the Torah scholar:

> *"Teacher, which is the great commandment in the law?" Jesus said to him, "'You shall love the LORD your God with all your heart, with all your soul, and with all your mind.' This is the first and great commandment. And the second is like it: 'You shall love your neighbor as yourself.' On these two commandments hang all the Law and the Prophets."* [214]

Right, back to the main argument…

The question posed by the Torah expert was in regard to life in the coming Kingdom of God with Messiah ruling from Jerusalem. With that understanding of *aionios* as meaning 'for the duration', it follows that 'eternal damnation' can just as

---

[213] Luke 10:28.

[214] Matthew 22:36-40.

easily mean 'for the duration of the [Messianic] age', however long that may be.[215]

In that light, consider the words of Yeshua as he describes the judgment that will take at the start of his messianic reign in the future. He describes the nations (i.e., gentiles) as divided in two – the righteous who cared for his brethren during persecution (on his right) and the wicked who did the opposite (on his left). He described their fate:

And these [on the left] *will go away into everlasting punishment, but the righteous* [to his right] *into eternal life.*

What is 'everlasting' punishment? The Greek word is our old friend *aionios*, the same word translated 'eternal' in describing the fate of the righteous. Why the translators would use different English words for the same Greek term that is a bit of a mystery. The cynic in me suggests that it is to underscore the awful nature of fire and brimstone forever and ever. However, the fact remains that the duration of life in the kingdom and life in punishment is identical.

Fire and Brimstone?

The notion of burning torment in Christian thought comes primarily from the symbolism in Revelation which describes Satan, the beast (the political component of the final evil empire, having failed in its attempt to destroy Israel) and the false prophet (its religious component) being cast into the Lake of Fire:

---

[215] As stated previously, the apocalyptic Book of Revelation states a thousand-year period. Jewish sources differ on the duration.

*The devil, who deceived them, was cast into the lake of fire and brimstone where the beast and the false prophet are. **And they will be tormented day and night forever and ever.***[216]

Here it is explicitly stated (at least in terms of the symbolism) that Satan, the beast and the false prophet will suffer eternal torment. As we've already seen, a few verses later, death and Sheol are cast into the burning lake, along with the irredeemably wicked. This is consistent with Second Temple Jewish thought:

*Then Death and Hades were cast into the lake of fire. This is **the second death**. And anyone not found written in the Book of Life was cast into the lake of fire.*[217]

It does not actually state that death, Sheol and the wicked are tormented day and night forever and ever. Given that death is a state and Sheol is a location, how could they be subjected to punishment? Instead, the text describes this final action as being 'the second death'. It is far more likely that final judgment which is *after* the millennial age,[218] will involve the non-existence of death and Sheol and annihilation for the incorrigible.

The other teaching in the Apostolic Writings used to affirm eternal punishment is recorded in the Gospel of Mark:

And if your eye causes you to sin, pluck it out. It is better for you to enter the kingdom of God with one eye, rather than having two eyes,

---

[216] Revelation 20:10, emphasis mine.

[217] Revelation 20:14–15, emphasis mine.

[218] Revelation 20:7.

to be cast into hell fire - where 'Their worm does not die and the fire is not quenched.'[219]

In the first place, Yeshua is using hyperbole – no righteous Jew would countenance self-mutilation – to underscore the importance of godly conduct. Secondly, the fate of the wicked is contrasted with the righteous who are granted entry into in the 'Kingdom of God'. Therefore, this fiery judgment will last for the duration of the kingdom. Finally, the last statement is a quote from the Book of Isaiah which describes the fate of the wicked during the Kingdom Age:[220]

*"And they shall go forth and look upon the **corpses** of the men who have transgressed against Me. For their worm does not die, and their fire is not quenched. They shall be an abhorrence to all flesh."* [221]

It's also worth a mention here that Second Temple Judaism believed in different levels of Gehinnom, according to the wickedness the individual displayed in his earthly existence.[222]

---

[219] Mark 9:47-48. This is the third warning in the passage; the previous two (verses 43-46) are identical, except the instrument of sin is first, the hand and then the foot, rather than the eye.

[220] That it is during the age of the kingdom is plain from the preceding verses in Isaiah.

[221] Isaiah 66:24, emphasis mine. Even if we were determined to stretch this punishment for all eternity, please note that the prophet does not refer to 'souls suffering eternal screaming anguish'. Rather, he refers to 'corpses' doubtless in reference to that historical practice in the Valley of Hinnom.

[222] In reference to David's grief following the death of Absalom, the Talmud states:

> *Why is 'my son' repeated eight times? Seven to raise him from the seven divisions of gehinnom; and for the last... to bring him into the world to come. (b.Sotah.10b)*

Whether that's so or not, most people would find that concept of Gehinnom as fair and reasonable.

On the other hand, whether it's true or not, most Christians (secretly) find the idea of everlasting torment for all and sundry who reject Yeshua as being unreasonable, and inconsistent with their knowledge of God.[223]

So, What's the Bottom Line?

It's simply that there is minimal difference in understanding, relating to the destiny of both the righteous and the wicked, between Second Temple Judaism and the Apostolic Writings if the latter are interpreted within the religious context of their writing.

The little elephant continues to shrink.

---

[223] Few will publicly admit to this secret heretical belief.

Chapter Four:
Naughty, Wicked Paul

Why is Paul such a controversial historical figure? While many Jews retain the idea that Yeshua was an evil man whose name daren't be uttered, most Jewish people today have some respect for him as a Jewish sage, misguided though he may have been, with the blame for the Christian religion being levelled at the workings of Paul.

The point of this chapter is to challenge the idea that Paul ruined an otherwise reasonable Jewish sect.[224] It is a nonsense that has resulted from misunderstanding on the part of Jews and some Christians as well.

But first, a little background information on the infamous apostle. Paul was something of a prodigy in Judaism who had advanced in understanding beyond his years. He said so himself, and you can't argue with fact like that, can you?

...I advanced in Judaism beyond many of my contemporaries in my own nation, being more exceedingly zealous for the traditions of my fathers.[225]

---

[224] Incidentally, it isn't just Jews who can have a negative attitude towards Paul the Apostle. I have heard him denigrated as being arrogant, misogynistic or legalistic at various times. As a pastor, on one occasion I quoted Paul during a disagreement with a lady, to make my point. Her response was, "Yes, but that's just Paul, and he's always over the top!" So, there you go.

[225] Galatians 1:14.

Although this may appear as an idle boast, Paul certainly had the right training. Hillel the Elder was a highly influential sage. He was the head of a school, the House of Hillel, which became the primary academy for Torah study prior to the destruction of the Second Temple.[226] His grandson Gamaliel was the first president of the Great Sanhedrin in Jerusalem and, according to Paul, this Gamaliel was the apostle's teacher. Under arrest in Jerusalem, he was granted permission to address a hostile Jewish crowd:

"Brethren and fathers, hear my defence before you now." And when they heard that he spoke to them in the Hebrew language, they kept all the more silent. Then he said: "I am indeed a Jew, born in Tarsus of Cilicia, but brought up in this city at the feet of Gamaliel, taught according to the strictness of our fathers' law, and was zealous toward God as you all are today." [227]

We have mentioned Paul's battle with the so-called 'super-apostles' in Corinth previously. These men were critical of Paul because he wasn't a 'real Jew' in their opinion. Paul's response was to defend his Jewish credentials in his second letter to Corinth:

Are they Hebrews? So am I. Are they Israelites? So am I. Are they the seed of Abraham? So am I.[228]

and also to the believers in Philippi:

---

[226] https://www.chabad.org/library/article_cdo/aid/4042931/jewish/Hillel-the-Elder.htm (accessed 29 July 2023).

[227] Acts 22:1-3.

[228] 2 Corinthians 11:22.

[I was] circumcised the eighth day, of the stock of Israel, of the tribe of Benjamin, a Hebrew of the Hebrews; concerning the law, a Pharisee...[229]

Some Christians erroneously believe that Paul 'converted' to Christianity and rejected his Jewishness. The reality is that Paul remained a Jew to the day of his death. In his defence before the Sanhedrin, he stated:

Men and brethren, I am a Pharisee, the son of a Pharisee; concerning the hope and resurrection of the dead I am being judged!" [230]

Additionally, by his own testimony, he remained Torah-observant. In Caesarea before the Roman Governor of Judea, Porcius Festus,[231] Paul avowed:

"Neither against the law of the Jews, nor against the temple, nor against Caesar have I offended in anything at all." [232]

and not long before his execution in Rome, Paul assured the Jewish leaders in that city that he had not transgressed any Jewish customs:

I have done nothing against our people or the customs of our fathers ...[233]

---

[229] Philippians 3:5.

[230] Acts 23:6b.

[231] Probably 'Porky' to his friends.

[232] Acts 25:8b.

[233] Acts 28:17b.

Paul's missionary activities followed a predictable pattern. He would proclaim his message, first in the local synagogues, of Yeshua as the crucified Messiah who would return in the future. This often earned him the right boot of fellowship accompanied by varying degrees of abuse and hatred. Christians assume that his rejection by the Jews of the Diaspora was because of his allegiance to a dead Nazarene whom he believed was the one to rule on David's throne.

Although that same message in today's synagogues would result in his rapid eviction from the premises, a careful reading of the Book of Acts reveals that his opponents' repudiation was primarily over a separate issue – the inclusion of the Gentiles in the salvific plan of God.

What's the big deal about Gentiles being saved? In the Tanakh, Isaiah prophesied the salvation of all Israel:

Also your people shall all be righteous; they shall inherit the land forever, the branch of My planting, the work of My hands, that I may be glorified.[234]

The conclusion from this text is that all Israel will have a place in the Age to Come, as recorded in the Mishnah:

---

[234] Isaiah 60:21. The first clause literally it reads: 'And your people all righteous'. The translators have added the future terms 'shall... be'. This is probably correct, since the previous refers to the day when Israel's mourning are concluded. During the Second Temple era, that may have been considered a present reality, since they were no longer in exile from the land. On the other hand, they were still under the oppression of Rome (Greece before that) and it could be argued that their mourning had not yet ceased.

All Israel have a portion in the world to come, for it is written: 'Thy people are all righteous; they shall inherit the land forever...[235]

My Jewish readers may be surprised to find that the Apostle Paul echoed this viewpoint, citing the Prophets and the Writings to support his position:[236]

And so all Israel will be saved, as it is written: "The Deliverer will come out of Zion, and He will turn away ungodliness from Jacob; for this is My covenant with them, when I take away their sins."[237]

While some have extrapolated the salvation of all Israel to infer that Gentiles are **excluded** from the messianic age,[238] most Jews (then and now) would accept that there is a place for Gentiles in the age to come.[239] The problem arose when Paul proclaimed that Gentiles were accepted under the New Covenant (which God promised exclusively to Israel and Judah) as **equals** with Jews. His basis was the promise to Abram in Genesis 12:3 regarding 'all the families of the earth.'

As you can imagine, this set the cat among the pigeons, not only because it was offensive to Jews, but the God-fearing gentiles attending the diasporic synagogues were falling over

---

[235] M.*Sanhedrin*.10:1. Note that the present tense has been assumed – see previous footnote.

[236] Isaiah 27:9; 59:21-21; Psalm 14:7.

[237] Romans 11:26-27.

[238] E.g. Rabbi Eliezer ben Hyrcanus in the Tosefta: t.*Sanhedrin*.13:2.

[239] Some of the kingdom prophecies in the Tanakh demand the existence of non-Jews e.g. Zechariah 14:17-18.

each other to join his bandwagon. For example, after Paul's lengthy sermon in the synagogue in Pisidian Antioch, the Book of Acts narrates:

So when the Jews went out of the synagogue, the Gentiles begged that these words might be preached to them the next Sabbath.[240]

Predictably, a large crowd gathered the following Saturday and the Jews felt obliged to draw a line in the sand, sending Paul away with a flea in his ear. The writer of Luke presents this in a Christian-biased manner, but there is doubtless some accuracy in his historical record of events, if not his description of it:

On the next Sabbath almost the whole city came together to hear the word of God. But when the Jews saw the multitudes, they were filled with envy; and contradicting and blaspheming, they opposed the things spoken by Paul.[241]

From that point on, the narrative of the Book of Acts reveals the enmity and vilification of Paul by his Jewish enemies until his death in Rome at the end of the book. Indeed, according to Acts, Paul was stoned and left for dead in Lystra but miraculously survived:

Then Jews from Antioch and Iconium came there; and having persuaded the multitudes, they stoned Paul and dragged him out of the city, supposing him to be dead. However, when the disciples gathered around him, he rose

---

[240] Acts 13:42.

[241] Acts 13:44-45.

up and went into the city. And the next day he departed with Barnabas to Derbe.[242]

The Apostle describes his other testing times – again in his defence against the super-apostles, after he assures his readers that he is as much a Hebrew as the pretenders were, he continues:

Are they ministers of Christ? – I speak as a fool – I am more: in labours more abundant, in stripes above measure, in prisons more frequently, in deaths often. From the Jews five times I received forty stripes minus one. Three times I was beaten with rods; once I was stoned; three times I was shipwrecked; a night and a day I have been in the deep; in journeys often, in perils of waters, in perils of robbers, in perils of my own countrymen, in perils of the Gentiles, in perils in the city, in perils in the wilderness, in perils in the sea, in perils among false brethren; in weariness and toil, in sleeplessness often, in hunger and thirst, in fastings often, in cold and nakedness – besides the other things, what comes upon me daily: my deep concern for all the churches. Who is weak, and I am not weak? Who is made to stumble, and I do not burn with indignation?[243]

So, What's the Bottom Line?

Paul was a devout Jew of the Pharisees and remained Torah-observant for his entire life. He was hated throughout the Greco-Roman world for proclaiming a message of Gentile inclusion in the Kingdom of God under the New Covenant

---

[242] Acts 14:19-20.

[243] 2 Corinthians 11:23-29.

that was promised to Israel. Even worse, he declared that Gentiles who responded to his message, would be equal to Jews in the age to come.

But that doesn't explain why, in some of his writings, he appears to encourage his readers to flout the commandments of God. How could a religious Jew do something like that?

Next chapter...

Chapter Five:
But Paul, You Said...

In his writings, Paul seems to make a number of antinomian statements. We won't look at them all because the explanation for all of them is the same, and since Paul's letter to Galatia is the primary 'go to' reference for the Torah-abolitionists, I'll restrict myself to just two common examples. Some interpret the first one below to say that keeping Torah[244] brings one under a curse:

> For as many as are of the works of the law are under the curse; for it is written, "Cursed is everyone who does not continue in all things which are written in the book of the law, to do them."[245]

In the second, Paul describes Torah as a 'tutor' whose function is to bring us to Yeshua, after which the tutor is no longer necessary:

> Therefore the law was our tutor to bring us to Christ, that we might be justified by faith. But after faith has come, we are no longer under a tutor.[246]

---

[244] As I mentioned way back, Torah means instruction but is translated in the Apostolic Writings by the Greek word νόμος (nomos). By the time it gets to English it is inaccurately rendered as 'law'.

[245] Galatians 3:10, citing Deuteronomy 27:26.

[246] Galatians 3:24-25.

The Apostle to Whom?

Just before we go any further, let's remind ourselves of what Paul believed his calling was. After fourteen years of acting as a lone wolf missionary to the Gentiles in the Diaspora, he went to Jerusalem to meet with the Jewish leadership of the Christian sect, accompanied by a fellow Jewish believer and a Gentile convert, Titus:

> *Then after fourteen years I went up again to Jerusalem with Barnabas, and also took Titus with* me.[247]

The reason for this meeting with the Jewish leaders was to receive their endorsement for his activities, as he continues in the next verse:

> *And I went up by revelation, and communicated to them that gospel which I preach among the Gentiles, but privately to those who were of reputation, lest by any means I might run, or had run, in vain.*[248]

Happily, for our apostle, the honchos in Jerusalem retained their calling to the Jews and approved his ministry to the Gentiles:

> *...they saw that the gospel for the uncircumcised had been committed to me, as the* gospel *for the circumcised was to Peter (for He who worked effectively in Peter for the apostleship to the circumcised also worked effectively in me toward the Gentiles), and when James, Cephas, and John, who seemed to be pillars, perceived the grace that*

---

[247] Galatians 2:1.

[248] Galatians 2:2.

had been given to me, they gave me and Barnabas the right hand of fellowship, that we should go to the Gentiles and they to the circumcised. They desired only that we should remember the poor, the very thing which I also was eager to do.[249]

Just to reiterate…

> ## PAUL WAS THE APOSTLE TO THE GENTILES – HIS WRITINGS ARE DIRECTLY PRIMARILY TOWARDS THEM.

Let's continue…

Must Gentiles Wear Tzitzit?

No, as I've already affirmed, Gentiles are born under the Noachide Covenant with its seven laws or four principles. Recall that this was the minimum standard set by the first Jewish followers of Yeshua, for entry into their religious group. It was understood that they would learn to obey more Torah as time went on.[250]

---

[249] Galatians 2:7b–10. Note that 'Cephas' is another name for 'Peter' who continued to proclaim Yeshua to the Jews, John (Yochanan) was Yeshua's closest friend and James (Ya'akov) was Yeshua's younger brother.

[250] Believe it or not, studies have shown that serious Christians comply with 78% of the mitzvot, compared to devout Jews at 100%. Three caveats must be applied to that figure:

1. It is based on those mitzvot that are applicable today. Not all can or need by complied with today. For example, some are only obligatory in the land; some are for priests only, and some are just for kings.

2. Not all Torah commandments are compatible with the judicial systems of our cultures e.g., the law of Levirate Marrige.

This is how it should be.

If I were to don a *kippah* and *tzitzit*,[251] it would be offensive to many religious Jews. I'd be pretending to be something that I'm not. There are mitzvot that specifically identify God's chosen people, distinguishing them from the rank and file. The downside is that this can potentially mark them out as objects of scorn and persecution.

The Apostle Paul's premise, as I've said, was based on the Abrahamic Covenant. He taught that Jews and Gentiles were to worship the one true God in unity and equality while retaining their respective ethnic identities.

More on that in a moment...

---

3. This only refers to the written Torah. Thus, a Christian can keep the dietary laws according to Leviticus and Deuteronomy but without meeting the requirements of Orthodox Judaism.

[251] For my Christian friends: skullcap and tassels. There are Christians who do this because, like some of Paul's opponents, believe (mistakenly, in my opion) that it's what God wants Gentiles to do.

Context is King

One of my favourite quotes, often attributed to the Christian scholar Don Carson,[252] goes like this:

A text without a context is a pretext for a proof text.

Do you like that? Whoever first coined this, whether Carson or somebody else, it's a great saying. And so it is that we must begin with the historical context that occasioned the writing of the letter to the Galatians.

The Christian assembly at Galatia was almost, if not entirely, comprised of Gentiles. However, just as it was the case in Corinth (and pretty much everywhere that Paul founded churches) false teachers had infiltrated their ranks after Paul moved on from the church he founded, having trained and appointed leaders. In Galatia, Paul referred to his enemies as 'the Judaizers'.[253] It is evident that, whoever these false teachers were,[254] they were insisting that Gentiles either complete a full conversion to Judaism, or that they keep all the mitzvot as if they hadn't done so.

This was attacking Paul's foundation of Jews and Gentiles together in unity and equality.

---

[252] With whom I disagree on many other issues!

[253] From the Greek word ἰουδαΐζω *(ioudaizo)*, meaning 'to become or live as a Jew.'

[254] In Antioch, they were religious Jews who advocated 'circumcision' i.e. full conversion (they weren't referring to simple the surgical procedure):

> *And certain men came down from Judea and taught the brethren, "Unless you are circumcised according to the custom of Moses, you cannot be saved." (Acts 15:1).*

Let's return to the first example of antinomianism above:

For as many as are of the **works of the law** *are under the curse; for it is written, "Cursed is everyone who does not continue in all things which are written in the book of the law, to do them."* [255]

What does he mean by the 'works of the law'?

Introducing 4QMMT

Despite the conspiracy theories attracted by the discovery of the Dead Sea Scrolls (DSS) and their non-disclosure to the public immediately, [256] the DSS played a huge part in confirming the veracity of the Hebrew text of the Tanakh and expanding scholars' knowledge of Second Temple Judaism.

One of these scrolls was 4QMMT. The number 4 signifies that it was discovered in cave number four and the Q specifies that it was found at Qumran. MMT is an abbreviation of its title: *Miqsat Ma'asei Ha-Torah*. Translated, this expression means, 'A Selection of the Works of the Law'. The document describes those things which identified the members of the ascetic Jewish sect at Qumran. [257]

In Paul-speak, the 'works of the law' are those things which specifically identify Jewish people. Paul's point in the passage, which he supports with the quote from Deuteronomy, is that

---

[255] Galatians 3:10, emphasis mine.

[256] It took many years of painstaking work to sort and reassemble all the fragments.

[257] Some have suggested that John the Baptist may have been a member of this sect.

Gentiles who display the identifying marks of a Jew are obliged to keep every jot and tittle of Torah and are cursed if they don't. An imperfect analogy would be,

> Don't wear the kepi of the French Foreign Legion unless you want to accept the legion's discipline.

Prior to the discovery of the DSS, most Christian expositors took the expression 'works of the law' to mean 'obedience to Torah'. On that basis, Jews who converted to Christianity were **expected** to reject their Jewishness and anything smacking of Judaism. As our American cousins say:

> Go figure.

What About the Redundant Tutor?

Here's the second sample text from Galatians, repeated for convenience:

> *Therefore the law was our tutor to bring us to Christ, that we might be justified by faith. But after faith has come, we are no longer under a tutor.*[258]

At first blush, this seems to be saying that Christians have Christ, therefore they don't need Torah any longer.

Like the rest of the letter to Galatia, this verse was meant to counter the Judaizers' insistence that the Gentile believers in that province were duty bound to keep all the mitzvot. The significant word in the passage is 'tutor'. It is the Greek word

---

[258] Galatians 3:24–25.

paidagogos. [259] In a well-to-do Roman household, the *paidagogos* was a slave whose responsibility was to escort a child safely to and from school and to teach him right from wrong, manners, customs and appropriate conduct.

Once the boy was of age, the slave would no longer be essential for the child had learned all the necessary lessons from the *paidagogos.* This did not mean that the young man could simply disregard all his lessons and live a vile life, without any consequences from his father! Similarly, Paul is saying that the Torah teaches us everything we need to know and, eventually, it has served its purpose in training **Gentiles**, who will be largely walking in a manner acceptable to God.[260]

But that doesn't explain how it could ever become redundant, does it? It only makes sense if the promised New Covenant is in effect at the present time. For under the New Covenant, Torah would be 'written on the hearts' of God's people who would be empowered by the spirit of God to walk in its statutes.

According to the Apostolic Writings (Jews feel free to disagree with what follows) the New Covenant was instituted at the death of Yeshua, as he said on the eve of his death at the Passover meal:

---

[259] παιδαγωγός – from which we get the English word 'pedagogue' – an instructor of children.

[260] It may be that 78% is a reasonable outcome from God's perspective for Gentiles since they lacked the benefit of being born under the Torah Covenant. Remember that Gentiles in the first century CE were vile pagans and cannot be compared with the average Joe, who grew up one of today's nations that were founded on Judeo-Christian ethics. And 78% is still likely to be a better standard that those Gentiles who remain under the Noachide principles.

And as they were eating, Jesus took bread, blessed and broke it, and gave it to them and said, "Take, eat; this is My body." Then He took the cup, and when He had given thanks He gave it to them, and they all drank from it. And He said to them, "This is My blood of the new covenant, which is shed for many." [261]

As I said, my Jewish readers are free to reject Yeshua's words, but they at least make sense of Paul's polemic against the Judaizers. He was simply sticking to his guns in his belief that Gentiles are not compelled to keep every single statute in the Torah. This especially applies to those uniquely Jewish statutes, the 'works of the law'.

So, What's the Bottom Line?

Gentiles are encouraged to keep Torah, and in practice they do keep nearly as many of the (written) mitzvot as Jews do. Paul resisted the efforts of the 'Judaizers' who demanded that Gentiles keep every jot and tittle of Torah because the foundation of the Apostle's ministry was the unity and equality of Jews and Gentiles without either group giving up their ethnic identities.

The Baby Elephant

Where does that leave the Borneo Baby? It is my considered opinion that this particular pygmy pachyderm is of little consequence to the relationship between Jews and Christians. Although there are different emphases between the

---

[261] Mark 14:22-24.

two faiths in regard to covenant, Torah, life after death and the place of Torah in the Gentile Christian's life, our two religions affirm basically the same things (that is, if the Apostolic Writings are interpreted through the lens of Second Temple Judaism).

That brings us now to the next lumbering beast, the Christian belief that Yeshua is the Messiah of Israel. Jews are more than free to reject that idea but, at the end of the day, does it mean that we can't still get along?

Let's find out..

Part Three: Middle-Sized Jumbo

Now we come to a more substantial difference of opinion dividing Jews and Christians. I do not propose to resolve it in this part of the book. That's because it is insoluble. Christians say Yeshua is the Messiah, Jews say he ain't, and ne'er the twain shall meet.

The primary reason for the animosity that still surrounds Yeshua's candidacy for the title is Christian ignorance of what

Messiah will do when he comes. Yes, Christians, **when** he comes. No, Christians, I'm not abandoning my belief that Yeshua is the Messiah of Israel. It will come as a shock to many Christians that, as I mentioned in the Introduction, Yeshua failed to fulfil all the messianic hopes of Judaism. Please Christians, don't run immediately for your prophetic proof-texts to the contrary, I beg of you. Those scriptures in the Tanakh that you hold dear to your

heart point to Yeshua as the fulfilment of Christian expectations of Messiah, and they're not the same as the Jewish ones from the Second Temple era (nor from today, for that matter).

My aim in this section is to put this matter behind us in a manner which causes minimal offence to both Jews and Christians. Whether I succeed or not will depend on the quantity of hate mail I receive from both camps!

To begin with, though, I have to justify my assertion that Yeshua didn't satisfy the messianic expectations of Israel. 'Tis a fairly simple thing to demonstrate that he didn't accomplish the things that **modern** Judaism demands of Messiah. A more difficult task is to determine exactly what the messianic assumptions of Jews in the Second Temple period were.

The first chapter in this part, of necessity, is devoted to listing the resources I used in determining Second Temple Jewish messianic hopes. Yes, more background stuff, I'm afraid. Once that's out of the way, I will endeavour to find a middle ground between Jews and Christians based on Yeshua's actual performance at the crease, despite his apparent dismal innings.[262]

---

[262] Don't give up on me just yet Christians, it's not quite as bad as it seems.

Chapter One:
Hitting the Source(s)

According to extensive research on my part,[263] the main expectations of the Jewish people today are that Messiah will:

1. Be a descendant of King David
2. Vanquish all of Israel's enemies
3. Restore all of Israel to the Promised Land (all of it – not just the tiny sliver they have today).
4. Rule from Jerusalem, the spiritual capital of the world.
5. Ensure Israel's obedience to Torah, as he correctly interprets it.

However, in the Second Temple period, the Jewish expectation was that Messiah would be identified by no less than *twenty-two* significant identifying actions, including the five listed above.

And how do I know that (I hear you ask)?

About ten years ago I completed a dissertation for my Doctor of Theology degree.[264] In published form it ran to around 150,000 words of boring academic-speak. The first half

---

[263] Okay, so that's a bit of an embellishment, I actually did a quick internet search…

[264] In fact, there were *over forty* messianic expectations in my dissertation, though most of them were inconsequential. See footnote at the end of next chapter for more on that.

was an attempt to establish precisely what Second Temple Messianic expectations were. To do that, I examined as much ancient Jewish literature as I could get my hands on.

What kind of literature (I hear you ask)?

Well, I'm glad you asked that question, because if I make claims about Yeshua's non-fulfilment of Judaism's ancient hopes, I'd better be able to back it up. What follows is an outline of the reference texts I used in
coming to that conclusion. If it gets to be hard going, skip to the next chapter where I will post the results obtained.

Where did you obtain those texts (I hear you ask)?

Sorry, no more questions. Just listen for now, okay?

What? Not Sola Scriptura?[265]

Obviously, the primary ancient Jewish source document is the Tanakh. Christians are adept at studying the Jewish bible, albeit in a back-to-front manner. What I mean by that is, beginning with the Apostolic Writings, they investigate the Tanakh to retrospectively prove the validity of the Apostolic Writings. To give you an example, having deduced a doctrine of trinitarianism from the Apostolic Writings, it is incumbent upon them to find allusions to it in the Tanakh by, if necessary,

---

[265] Mentioned in a previous chapter, means 'scripture alone'. Believe it or not, it takes biblical inferences – not just the plain texts – to prove *'sola scriptura'*. Just one of those little ironies of church history, I suppose.

employing an ancient theological technique known as jiggery-pokery.[266]

As a corollary,[267] we modern Greek-thinkers delve for different information from scripture than did the ancient Hebrew-thinkers who authored it. The Apostle Paul, in his first letter to assembly at Corinth wrote:

For Jews request a sign, and Greeks seek after wisdom…[268]

Permit me to illustrate the perspicacity of that ancient observation.

---

[266] Coincidentally, this is the name of a most unusual card game played while performing an old Irish dance.

[267] A small, but popular, Japanese car mass-produced by Toyota.

[268] 1 Corinthians 1:22.

Greeks Seek After Wisdom

Conservative Gentile Christians argue that the creation account is an intentional scientific treatise of how the universe came into being, insisting that God created the world in six 24-hour periods. Other strive to reconcile the creation narrative with scientific thought by employing the 'long creation days' theory.[269]

Is that the purpose of the creation narrative?

Jews Request a Sign

The second verse of Genesis states:

And the Spirit of God was hovering over the face of the waters.[270]

Consider the ancient Jewish perspective on this verse:

This alludes to the spirit of Messiah, as you read 'And the Spirit of the Lord shall rest upon him' (Isa XI, 2). In the merit of what will [this spirit] eventually come? [For the sake of that which] hovered over the face of the waters, i.e. the merit of repentance which is likened to water, as it is written, 'pour out thy heart like water' (Lam. II, 19). "[271]

---

[269] That is, the six creation 'days' really refer to very long periods, perhaps millions of years. Canadian astrophysicist and author Hugh Ross holds this viewpoint e.g. Ross, *Creation and Time* (Carol Stream: 2004).

[270] Genesis 1:2b.

[271] *Bereshit Rabbah 1.2*. This book, written probably around the 4th century CE is a Talmudic midrash on the Book of Genesis – a commentary applying the exegetical patterns of the ancient sages.

This explanation, totally at odds with Greek thinking, is nonetheless accordant with the ancient Hebraic approach.[272]

In investigating the Tanakh for glimpses of *Jewish* messianic expectations, it seemed appropriate to allow *their* ancient interpretations of the texts to be the source. And this is a convenient time to introduce some of my Christian readers to the word 'Targum'.[273]

Don't Forget the Targums, Mum[274]

During their time in exile, the Jews adopted the Aramaic tongue of their captors.[275] Exiled teachers, familiar with the written Hebrew texts[276] would recite the bible from memory to the those born in exile (who had lost their native language) in Aramaic. In the process, the teachers added extra commentary or explanation.[277] Later, these Aramaic versions of the scriptures were written down in the adopted language,

---

[272] e.g. The Seven Rules of Interpretation formulated by Hillel in the first century BCE Bacher & Lauterbach, *Jewish Encyclopedia,* http://www.jewishencyclopedia.com/view.jsp? artid =472&letter=R. (accessed 14 July 20230.This example is in line with Hillel's second rule, *G'zerah Shavah.*

[273] Despite the name, it isn't a chewable nicotine substitute.

[274] If you can remember the original commercial from which that subtitle is plagiarised, you're way too old! Oh, by the way, the technically correct plural of targum is *targumim.*

[275] They also adopted the Chaldean (Aramaic) alphabet for use with the Hebrew language. This is not to suggest that their grasp of the Hebrew language was completely lost, as some have suggested.

[276] Complete memorisation of the Torah was common.

[277] Similar to a commentary or 'study bible'. The difference is that the 'gloss' is within the biblical text itself. Some say that while in exile, those still skilled in Hebrew, would translate the Tanakh into Aramaic as they read the text for those born in exile who could only speak Aramaic.

including the added commentary, known as 'gloss'. The gloss, though not of divine inspiration, reveals the commonly held interpretation of the Tanakh from that era and taken at face value, supplies a treasure trove of messianic hopes not clear from a straightforward reading of the Tanakh.

Two major "Eastern" Targums originated in Babylon. The first is *Targum Onqelos.*[278] The second is called *Targum Jonathan* and is the

Aramaic translation of the Nevi'im (prophets) written by Jonathan ben Uzziel.[279] He was a student of the great Jewish sage, Hillel the Elder.[280]

Most books of the Ketuvim (writings) also have Aramaic translations which are less well-preserved than the rest and are more difficult to date, since they are not mentioned in the Talmud.[281]

The Western Targums originated in the land of Israel. This is reflected in their group title *Targum Yerushalmi.*[282] The

---

[278] Onqelos (also spelled 'Onkelos') was a Roman convert to Judaism in the late first-century CE. According to Talmud his Aramaic translation of the Torah was completed under the guidance of two well-accredited Rabbis, Eleazar and Joshua (b.*Megilah.*3a). Apparently, he was also known as *Aquila.*

[279] b.*Megilah.*3a.

[280] Died c. 10 CE. His grandson, Gamaliel gets a couple of mentions in the Apostolic Writings. His wisdom is revealed in Acts 5:34 and the Apostle Paul claims that Gamaliel was his teacher in Acts 22:3.

[281] Generally considered to have been written in the sixth to eighth centuries CE. I apportioned a little less weight to these documents, due to their relatively late authorship.

[282] Alternatively called the 'Palestinian Targum', based on the name of the Holy Land since the second century CE. However, because of the political association of

largest is the Aramaic translation of the Torah from this region called the *Targum Neofiti*.[283] There are also twelve fragmentary Targums from the west which, for a period, were called *Targum Yerushalmi II*. These are now known by their individual fragment names.[284]

There was a wealth of messianic information contained within the Targums and these make up the bulk of the expectations in the list at the beginning of the next chapter. Worthy of special mention though, is the
belief in two messiahs: the Son of Joseph and the Son of David.[285] Curiously, this dynamic duo rates a mention in the Talmud.[286]

Apocrypha on Both Your Houses!

The Apocrypha are a collection of Jewish texts from the period of the Second Temple. They contained a few minor insights into the messianic expectations of those times.

---

terms related to historic Palestine, I prefer the qualifier 'Yerushalmi'. Another version of this Targum was incorrectly associated with Jonathan ben Uzziel and named *Targum Jonathan*. In view of this mistake, it is still known as *Targum Pseudo-Jonathan*.

[283] This Targum was kept in the Vatican for centuries and only rediscovered in the 1956 by a Spanish Catholic priest and scholar, Alejandro Diez Macho (1916–1984), a fairly butch chap as his name implies. It is very similar to Targum Pseudo-Jonathan.

[284] Assigned various letters of the alphabet to distinguish them: A through H, L, P, V & Z.

[285] Tg.Cant 4:5.

[286] In b.*Sukkah*.52b, two of the four craftsmen seen in Zechariah 1:20-21 are identified as the two Messiahs – the Sons of Joseph and David. In *Sukkah*.52a, eternal life is granted at the behest of Messiah Son of David, following the death of Messiah Son of Joseph.

The Book of Baruch

The Book of Baruch purports to be written by the friend and secretary of the Major Prophet Jeremiah, Baruch the son of Neriah. His name appears over twenty times in the Book of Jeremiah. Modern scholarship disputes the authorship and attributes its composition to a later time – the second century BCE. Although it doesn't have any direct references to the Messiah, it does contain an allusion to a time in the future, when the destruction of Israel's enemies is anticipated.

The Book of Tobit

The Book of Tobit was probably penned in the late third century BCE, though set several centuries earlier in the Assyrian captivity. It is a beautifully written story of suspense and morality. It contains a petition to God to judge the oppressors of his people. Within this petition is the inference of the gentile nations coming to Jerusalem to worship the God of Israel.

The Book of Sirach

Although the Book of Sirach contains some themes harmonious with Second Temple Jewish messianic hope, I was obliged to reject it based on the Talmudic injunction to do so:

"R. Joseph said: it is . . . forbidden to read the book of Ben Sira."[287]

---

[287] b.*Sanhedrin*.100b.

The Books of Maccabees

There is but one oblique reference to messianic concepts in the Books of Maccabees. The dying Mattathias, in his final speech, describes how Israel's past heroes received reward for their loyalty to law and covenant. In so doing, he makes mention of the eternal nature of the Davidic dynasty.[288]

Sued a What?

The term 'pseudepigrapha' is applied to documents written from the third century BCE to the third century CE. They are highly unlikely to have been written by the authors' names attributed to them.[289]

Psalms of Solomon

The Psalms of Solomon were composed by a Zadokite priest living in Jerusalem following the Maccabean revolt in the second century BCE. These texts revealed four prominent aspects of the Messiah's anticipated ministry, namely, the time

---

[288] 1 Maccabees 2:50-51,57.

[289] Copyright laws have changed since those days. I know this because when I originally submitted this book for publication, it was rejected on the basis that J.K. Rowling clearly hadn't written it. Oh well, it was worth a try.

of his coming,[290] his origin,[291] his mission[292] and the character of his rule.[293]

The Book of 2 Baruch

This book, also known as the [Syrian] Apocalypse of Baruch, claims to be another revelation given to Baruch ben Neriah. Scholars believe it to be written by a Torah–observant Jew in response to the destruction of the Temple in 70 CE, though some believe the final ten chapters were written later – early second century CE. Several sections contain messianic references to themes found in the Tanakh and Targums, including the conditions preceding Messiah's return; the resurrection of the dead; Messiah's judgment of Jews *and* Gentiles,[294] and the restoration of planet earth.[295]

And now for something completely different – a passage within the book claims that when Messiah comes, the great beasts Leviathan and Behemoth will be slain to provide a banquet for the people of God.[296]

---

[290] Ps.Sol 17:23.

[291] *Ibid.*

[292] Ps.Sol 17:24–27,50.

[293] Ps.Sol 17:31,41.

[294] The latter according to the Noachide Covenant.

[295] 2 Baruch 25:3; 29:3-5; 30:1-2; chapters 50-51; 68:1-5; 70:9-71:1; 72:2-5; 73:1-8.

[296] Dining on monster mash is also attested in the midrash to Leviticus – *Vayikra Rabbah 32:10*. Nevertheless, given its infrequent mention, I did not include this in the general list of Jewish Messianic expectations.

The Apocalypse of Ezra

Also referred to as either '2 Esdras' or '4 Ezra', this book describes the destruction of Jerusalem and Solomon's Temple at the hands of the Babylonian invaders in the sixth century BCE[297] although it is thought to have been written in the first century CE following the destruction of the *Second* Temple. In this writing, the author seeks to understand why the Romans[298] were still enjoying their prosperity while the Jews continued in their suffering.[299]

A disappointing feature of extant copies of 4 Ezra is that the evidence points to Christian authorship of the first two and the final two chapters.[300] Despite this evident scribal meddling, 4 Ezra does contain references to the Messiah and the Age to Come, even if only the middle twelve chapters of the apocalypse are considered. The only messianic prediction not found in other literature is that Messiah will only live for four hundred years.[301]

---

[297] 4 Ezra 10:21.

[298] Referred to as 'Babylonians'.

[299] A little like the biblical Book of Habakkuk.

[300] There are references to 'Jesus' in the latter portion and it's highly unlikely that the original Jewish author would have done so.

[301] 4 Ezra 7:28-29; 12:31-34. The lifespan of Messiah is not confirmed in any of the other sources I examined, so I didn't give much credence to this prophetic idea either.

The Book of Jubilees

The Book of Jubilees[302] is a fifty-chapter work from the second century BCE and is a retelling of Genesis and the first twenty chapters of Exodus given to Moses by an angel during his ascension. There is a passage within which describes the familiar themes of Messiah ruling over a kingdom of peace, freed from Gentile oppression.[303]

The Book of Enoch

The Book of Enoch, also known as '1 Enoch'[304] was composed by several authors during the third to the first centuries BCE. Within are a significant number of messianic references, most notably in the second subsection called the *Book of Similitudes*.[305] The book confirms several of the messianic expectations encountered in other writings[306] and introduces two ideas not directly found elsewhere: the identification of Messiah as Isaiah's 'Branch from Jesse,'[307] and the messianic title 'son of man', also seen in the Book of Daniel.[308]

---

[302] Also referred to as 'Lesser Genesis'.

[303] Jubilees 31:18-20a.

[304] To distinguish it from a later work, the Secrets of Enoch. As an aside, the Book of Enoch is the only pseudepigraphal book directly quoted within the Apostolic Writings - 1 Enoch 1:9 is quoted in Jude 14-15.

[305] 1 Enoch chapters 37-81

[306] 1 Enoch 1:3b,9a; 38:1-2, 5-6; 39:6-7a; 45:3-6; 46:4-6. 48:5; 51:1-3; 52:2-9; 53:2b,6; 61:5,8-11; 62:1-2; 63:11; 69:26-29; 71:14-17.

[307] 1 Enoch 49:2b-4 cp. Isaiah 11:1-5.

[308] 1 Enoch 48:10. This expression simply means 'human being' and appears many times in that sense in the Book of Ezekiel. However, in Daniel 7:13 the phrase

The final section of Enoch, *The Epistle of Enoch,* is a mixed bag comprised of several smaller, and often out-of-sequence parts including the *Apocalypse of Weeks,* (which narrates the history of the world; an exhortation supposedly from Enoch to his son Methuselah; an epistle regarding the righteous and the wicked and their respective fates and a narrative on the Birth of Noah. Although some of the messianic themes found earlier in the Book of Enoch can be discerned in the Book of Noah,[309] direct messianic allusions are absent.

Not Only, But Also...

I think I'll wrap this chapter up fairly swiftly now – lest I fall asleep myself! But here's the rest of the ancient documents I examined to arrive at the list posted at the end of this chapter.

The Syballine Oracles

The so-called 'Sibylline Oracles' are a collection of ancient writings comprising fifteen books of supposed prophecy thought to have been composed by both Jews and Christians between the second century BC and the fourth century CE. Book Three of the Sibylline collection contains a significant amount of Jewish material which describes primeval history, reviews a series of worldly empires and sketches the nature, history and future of the Jewish people, including several

---

appears in the context of one 'coming with the clouds of heaven' – clearly a messianic reference.

[309] e.g. resurrection: 1 Enoch 91:10; the salvation of the righteous: 1 Enoch 91:14; 99:10, and destruction of the wicked: 1 Enoch 97:1 etc.

prophecies of a messianic nature. The only one of interest is the prediction that the Messiah would come when Egypt was subjugated by Rome,[310] a portent not supported elsewhere in the ancient texts.

The Writings of Josephus

The writings of Flavius Josephus[311] are surprisingly lacking in historical reference to the messianic expectation of first-century Judaism. A solitary example can be found in his *Wars of the Jews*, in which he explains that the Jewish motivation for the uprising against the Romans in the first century was, in part, their anticipation of a world ruler arising from among their ranks.[312]

The Dead Sea Scrolls

In contrast to the works of Josephus, there are several messianic references in the Dead Sea Scrolls, which can be found in both their community manuscripts and Biblical commentaries. Although they contribute little in the way of innovative information, they serve to reinforce Second Temple messianic expectations. Interestingly, they also identify more than one individual in the role of Messiah,[313]

---

[310] Sib. Or. 3:46-49.

[311] 37–c.101 CE, was born Yoseph ben Mattityahu in Jerusalem to a priestly family.

[312] War of the Jews 6.V.4.

[313] 1QSa 2:11-21; 1QS 9:7-11; CD 14:19; Having said that, most of the messianic passages in the scrolls deal primarily with the Son of David e.g., 1QM 5:1; 4Q504

although they tend to differentiate between a Warrior–King (à la David) and a Messiah who will function as a righteous priest. Doubtless they anticipated that the latter would remove the priesthood from Jerusalem, whom the Qumran community saw as corrupt.

So, What's the Bottom Line?

Thank you, you've been very patient through this last chapter (at least most of you have!). Its purpose was to give some credibility to the list of ancient messianic expectations from the Second Temple period and thereabouts.

Here now is the list of criteria which would identify Messiah when he came from the same era as when Yeshua conducted his ministry. The first five have continued through to the present era as messianic hopes.

1. Land restored to Israel

2. Obedience to Torah

3. Ruling from Jerusalem

4. Davidic descent

5. Vanquish Israel's enemies

---

6. Messiah on the clouds if Israel is worthy

7. Messiah on an ass if Israel is unworthy

4:5-8; 1QSb 5:20-25. Other references link the Messiah to the branch of Jesse prophecy in Isaiah 11 e.g. 4Q285 Frag.5; 4QpIsa 3:18-22.

8. The return of the Shekinah

9. Restoration of the earth to a pristine state

10. Salvation for Gentiles

11. Messiah will judge the Gentile nations

12. Transfer of wealth of the gentile nations

13. Division of the land among the tribes of Israel

14. Global peace

15. A time of travail prior to Messiah's arrival

16. Messiah's appearance heralded by Elijah

17. Two Messiahs: the Son of Joseph who will be slain, and

18. Messiah, the Son of David who will rule over Israel

19. Resurrection of the dead

20. Messiah accompanied by an entourage

21. Messiah is the Son of Man

22. The Son of Man is pre-existent.

What do we do with all this? If we want to be generous, we can accredit Yeshua with a small handful of the criteria listed above. Yes, he was born of the line of David as we noted previously.[314] Of the additional markers that I drew from the texts mentioned in this chapter, taking the Apostolic Writings at face value (as I did with all the other ancient Jewish texts):

---

[314] An Orthodox Jewish friend pointed out that, since Christians believe in the virgin birth of Yeshua, that disqualifies him as a descendant of David. Do with that what you wish.

1. He did arrive on a donkey.
2. He claimed to be the Son of Man
3. He was slain as Messiah the Son of Joseph.
4. He brought a measure of salvation to the Gentiles (again according to the Apostolic Writings).

Including his Davidic lineage, that's a grand total of 5 out of 22 ancient Jewish messianic criteria.

To my beloved Christian readers, does that help you to understand why those Jewish folks, who are familiar with the Tanakh,[315] are unimpressed with, for example, Isaiah chapter fifty-three?

Am I telling you dear Christians that we are simply barking up the wrong tree?

Stay tuned…

---

[315] Sadly, like most Christians, most Jews are not all that familiar with what the bible actually says.

Chapter Two:
Missed it by that Much?[316]

Last chapter we concluded that Yeshua only fulfilled five out of the twenty-two ancient and modern messianic hopes. By this point (if they haven't already given up on me), a large percentage of my Christian readers will be engaging in the ancient biblical practice of gnashing of teeth. To that end, I need to lay my cards on the table and reassure them that I haven't gone completely loopy.[317] Lest I be accused of a hidden missionary agenda, I will now attempt to reassure my fellow followers of Yeshua.

Jews may cover the ears for the next few paragraphs while we get this out of the way. But please make sure you read the summary at the end of this chapter prior to preceding – that will ensure we're all on the same wavelength prior to continuing.

First of all, we have to answer the question…

Did Yeshua Claim to be Messiah?

On trial for his life, Yeshua was asked this very question:

---

[316] Acknowledging that this expression is plagiarised from Agent 86, Maxwell Smart.

[317] No, I haven't. Well, at least not *completely* loopy.

And the high priest stood up in the midst and asked Jesus, saying, "Do You answer nothing? What is it these men testify against You?" But He kept silent and answered nothing. But Jesus kept silent. And the high priest answered and said to Him, "I put You under oath by the living God: Tell us if You are the Christ, the Son of God!" [318]

Yes, But Not Today...

It was certainly in Yeshua's interest to 'plead the fifth' at his trial, irrespective of how he viewed his mission. Nonetheless, Matthew's account of the high priest's interrogation provides an additional detail, not mentioned by Mark:

But Jesus kept silent. And the high priest answered and said to Him, **"I put You under oath by the living God:** *Tell us if You are the Christ, the Son of God!"* [319]

Based on the framing of the High Priest's question, Yeshua acquiesced (as the next verse affirms) with the foreseeable result:

Jesus said, "I am. And you will see the Son of Man sitting at the right hand of the Power, and coming with **the clouds of heaven**. *" Then the high priest tore his clothes and said, "What further need do we have of witnesses? You have heard the blasphemy! What do you think?" And they all condemned Him to be deserving of death.* [320]

---

[318] Mark 14:60–61a.

[319] Matthew 26:63, emphasis mine.

[320] Matthew 26:64–66, emphasis mine.

On what basis could this man make such an outrageous affirmation, given that his lifespan was now numbered in hours?

All my readers will be aware that Apostolic Writings attest that Yeshua rose from the dead on the third day following his execution. This was something that he himself predicted would happen on many occasions.[321]

Whether the resurrection of Yeshua is a historic fact (or otherwise) is outside the scope of this book. Of greater significance is what he, and the authors of the Apostolic Writings affirmed about the twenty-two messianic expectations of Second Temple Judaism.

To put it simply, Yeshua and his early followers explicitly or implicitly **confirmed every one** of the twenty-two ancient Jewish messianic hopes. We've already seen one example. Yeshua, in predicting his coming with the clouds of heaven, endorsed the Jewish belief in the arrival of Messiah on the clouds when Israel is worthy. His coming on an ass reveals (at least) his opinion that the time was not appropriate for the establishment of the Kingdom of God around 30 CE.

The Restoration of Israel

Let's consider another example or two before we move on. For simplicity we will confine our study to just the first book in the Apostolic Writings: The Gospel of Matthew. However,

---

[321] Plainly in Matthew 16:21–23, 33; 17:22–23; 20:17–19; Mark 8:31–32; 9:30–32; 10:32-34; Luke 9:21-22, 43-45; 18:31-34. More subtly in John 12:7-8; 13:33; 14:25.

all the authors of the Apostolic Writings endorse the Second Temple Messianic beliefs.

It is evident that Yeshua believed that he would, at his return, rule over a restored Israel. In the text below, he refers to the messianic era as the 'regeneration':

> *So Jesus said to them, "Assuredly I say to you, that in the regeneration, when the Son of Man sits on the throne of His glory, you who have followed Me will also sit on twelve thrones, judging the twelve tribes of Israel.* [322]

His mention of the 'twelve tribes' also demands the reunification of the northern and southern kingdoms.

Torah in the Messianic Age

We've pretty much hashed it to death, but many Christians believe that Yeshua abolished Torah. In fact, the opposite is true. In the following passage he distinctly says that obedience to even the lesser commandments will decide one's status in the messianic kingdom:

> *For assuredly, I say to you, till heaven and earth pass away, one jot or one tittle will by no means pass from the law till all is fulfilled. Whoever therefore breaks one of the least of these commandments, and teaches men so, shall be called least in the kingdom of heaven; but whoever does and*

---

[322] Matthew 19:28.

teaches them, he shall be called great in the kingdom of heaven. [323]

Furthermore, in explaining one of his parables to his disciples, he declares that those who are 'torah-less' will be removed from the Kingdom of God:

The Son of Man will send out His angels, and they will gather out of His kingdom all things that offend, and those who practice **lawlessness**, *and will cast them into the furnace of fire. There will be wailing and gnashing of teeth. Then the righteous will shine forth as the sun in the kingdom of their Father. He who has ears to hear, let him hear!* [324]

The Footsteps of Messiah

Yeshua prophesied at length on events that would precede the coming of the Messiah. Christians will be familiar with the discourse he gave on the Mount of Olives, but the passage is repeated below for any Jewish readers who may be unfamiliar with Yeshua's take on the time of travail that would take place in the last days. Please note that he corrects the notion that Messiah could come 'on the quiet', as it were. There will be no doubt in anybody's mind when the Son of David comes to rule:[325]

---

[323] Matthew 5:18-19. For my Christian readers, the expression 'Kingdom of Heaven' does not mean 'heaven'. It is a circumlocution for the Kingdom of God – in deference to Jewish sensibilities about excessive use of the word 'God'. It means the age to come when Messiah rules on David's throne from Jerusalem.

[324] Matthew 13:41-43.

[325] It is my belief that these events are centred in Israel and the surrounding nations – not worldwide cataclysms as some Christians teach.

And Jesus answered and said to them: "Take heed that no one deceives you. For many will come in My name, saying, 'I am the Christ,' and will deceive many. And you will hear of wars and rumors of wars. See that you are not troubled; for all these things must come to pass, but the end is not yet. For nation will rise against nation, and kingdom against kingdom. And there will be famines, pestilences, and earthquakes in various places. All these are the beginning of sorrows. Then they will deliver you up to tribulation and kill you, and you will be hated by all nations for My name's sake. [10] And then many will be offended, will betray one another, and will hate one another. Then many false prophets will rise up and deceive many. And because lawlessness will abound, the love of many will grow cold. But he who endures to the end shall be saved. And this gospel of the kingdom will be preached in all the world as a witness to all the nations, and then the end will come. Therefore when you see the 'abomination of desolation,' spoken of by Daniel the prophet, standing in the holy place" (whoever reads, let him understand), "then let those who are in Judea flee to the mountains. Let him who is on the housetop not go down to take anything out of his house. And let him who is in the field not go back to get his clothes. But woe to those who are pregnant and to those who are nursing babies in those days! And pray that your flight may not be in winter or on the Sabbath. For then there will be great tribulation, such as has not been since the beginning of the world until this time, no, nor ever shall be. And unless those days were shortened, no flesh would be saved; but for the elect's sake those days will be shortened. Then if anyone says to you, 'Look, here is the Christ!' or 'There!' do not believe it. For false christs and false prophets will rise and show great signs and wonders to deceive, if possible, even the elect. See, I have told you beforehand. Therefore if they say to you, 'Look, He is in the desert!' do not go out; or 'Look, He is in the inner rooms!' do not believe it. For as the lightning comes from the east and flashes to the west, so also will the coming of the Son of Man be. [326]

So, What's the Bottom Line?

Honestly, I could go on and on, demonstrating the endorsement of the Apostolic Writings for all things Jewish and messianic. But there seems no point in doing that – surely it would become boring.[327]

---

[326] Matthew 24:4–27.

[327] Okay, point taken. How about *more* boring? But just for the record, here's the seventeen ancient Jewish messianic expectations, unfulfilled by Yeshua at his coming and some references from the Apostolic Writings which either confirm, prophetically reveal, or at least infer that these hopes will be fulfilled at his return:

1. Messiah on the clouds if Israel is worthy (Matthew 24:30; 26:64; Mark 14:62); 2. Messiah on an ass if Israel is unworthy (Matthew 21:2-7; John 12:14-15); 3. The return of the Shekinah (Matthew 17:5; Mark 9:7; Luke 17:34-35; 2 Peter 1:16-18); 4. Restoration of the earth to a pristine state (Acts 3:20-21 Romans 8:19-25; 2 Peter 3:13; Revelation 22:3-5); 5. Salvation for Gentiles (Matthew 28:19-20; Mark 16:15; Luke 24:47-48; Acts 1:8; 10:34-43; most letters of Paul); 6. Messiah will judge the Gentiles (Matthew 25:31-44); 7. Transfer of wealth of the gentile nations (Matthew 2:9-12 typology); 8. Division of the land among the tribes of Israel (Matthew 19:28; Revelation 21:12-14); 9. Global peace (Luke 2:14; John 16:33); 10. A time of travail prior to Messiah's arrival (Matthew 24:4-36; Mark 13:5-23; Luke 21:5-24 Revelation 6:9-11; 7:14); 11. Messiah's appearance heralded by Elijah (Matthew 17:10-11; Mark 9:11-12); 12. Messiah Son of Joseph who will be slain (Matthew 27:50; Mark 15:37-38; Luke 23:46; John 19:30; Acts 2:36; 1 Corinthians 15:3; 1 Thessalonians 4:14; etc.); 13. Messiah Son of David who will rule over Israel (Matthew 1:1; 19:28; 25:31; Luke 1:32; 3:23-31; Acts 1:6-7; 2:30); 14. Resurrection of the dead Acts 23:6,8; 26:6-8; 1 Corinthians 6:14; 15:20-23; 1 Thessalonians 4:14; Hebrews 6:2; Revelation 20:4-6); 15. Messiah accompanied by an entourage (Matthew 25:31; Mark 8:38; 1 Thessalonians 3:12-13; Jude 14); 16. Messiah is the Son of Man (Matthew 1:5-6; Matthew 26:64; Mark 14:62; Luke 9:26; 21:27; John 5:26-27; Acts 7:56; 13:22-23; Romans 15:2; Revelation 1:14; 13:13). 17. The Son of Man is pre-

Here's the punchline:

From a Christian perspective, Yeshua fulfilled the prophecies of Messiah, the Son of Joseph, who would suffer for his people. At his return, he will fulfil the prophecies of Messiah, the Son of David.

What it boils down to [and please, this is important] the only thing that should separate Jews and Christians regarding the Messiah is that, if Christians are right, the Messiah may well say:

"You know, Jerusalem has changed since I was here last time."

That is, if Christians are right, his name will be Yeshua of Nazareth. If Christians are wrong, his name will be something else – perhaps Abe Cohen of Caulfield.

That's it, people. That's what divides us on the person of Messiah ben David who will do all the things that both ancient and modern Judaism expects of him.

Do we really need to sort it out with swords or pistols?

Why have Christians pushed Yeshua as the ***Jewish*** Messiah who came once 2000 years ago, and now rules from heaven

---

existent (John 1:2-3,15-18; 3:13; 8:58-59; 17:5,24; Colossians 1:16-17; Hebrews 1:2; 1 Peter 1:20).

As mentioned in footnote in the previous chapter, there were actually over forty messianic expectations in my research. I left them most of them out of this book to avoid causing catalepsy in my readers. But, if you're wondering, the Apostolic Writings confirms **all of them** – Michael J. Rowles, *To the Jew First: Restoring the Evangel to the Context of Hebraic Antiquity,* dissertation for the award of Doctor of Theology, (Louisiana: LBTS, 2013).

without having to accomplish all the things that *Jews* expects of him?

To pinch one of the Apostle Paul's sayings and use it out of context, regarding my Christian brothers and sisters:

For I bear them witness that they have a zeal for God, but not according to knowledge.[328]

Mama Mammoth

Our Indian elephant, correctly understood, boils down to a difference of opinion. Yeshua did not achieve the messianic expectations of Judaism. Christianity has ignored that reality claiming different goals for *Israel's* messiah(!).

The fact is that, when Mashiach comes, he will do all that the Tanakh predicted and all that the Jewish people – ancient and modern – expect of him.

At the end of the day, we are quibbling about his name. Like I said in the beginning, we say 'Yeshua', you say 'potato'. Get over it please, both groups.

So the midsize mammoth is a reality but shouldn't bring divisive animosity any longer (acknowledging the historic antisemitism of the Christian church and the hatred it displayed towards Jews in the name of whom they believed to be the Jewish Messiah). Hopefully, times have changed.

And that just leaves us with the big fella, the Trinity.

---

[328] Romans 10:42.

This is the tricky bit...

Part Four:
The Three-in-One Elephant

Photo: Sam Mann - Upsplash

We have put away the pygmy pachyderm; moved beyond the middle-sized mammoth, and now it's time to tackle the titanic tusker.

What's a Trinity?

For those Jewish readers who may be unfamiliar with the Christian belief in the Trinity, it is this: there is one God who consists of three equal persons. Those three are God the Father; God the Son (Jesus), and God the Holy Spirit. These three are different from one another, but together, make up the one true God.

As I mentioned in the introduction to this book, that belief creates both philosophical and mathematical difficulties – the latter arises especially as Christians attempt to defend against allegations of tritheism.

So, here's what I propose…

Both Jewish and Christian readers should read to the end of this introduction to chapter one. Jewish readers may continue out of intellectual curiosity to see the foundation upon which trinitarian belief rests – such as it is. My Jewish readers who find that the rest of this section is offensive to them, may skip to the 'bottom line' paragraphs at the end of the five chapters that constitute this part of the book. Christian readers would do well to read the entire section to gain a better grip on their own beliefs, in order to consider an alternative viewpoint from a position of understanding.

Right, let's get into it…

There are 7,957 verses in the Apostolic Writings. The three 'persons' of the trinity appear together in just *one verse* in the Apostolic Writings. It's when Yeshua instructed his Jewish followers to make converts of the gentiles. Those converts would have to undergo a mikveh, and walk in obedience to his teachings:

*Go therefore and make disciples of all the nations, baptising them in the name of the **Father** and of the **Son** and of the*

Holy Spirit, *teaching them to observe all things that I have commanded you....*[329]

Some have criticised this passage as being a later interpolation, on the basis that when Peter passed on this message to a group of several thousand Jews (gathered in Jerusalem for *Shavuot)*, he said:

...Repent, and let every one of you be baptized in the name of Jesus Christ for the remission of sins...[330]

Still, in this book so far, I've endeavoured to take texts at 'face value'. Let's leave it to others to debate what the original manuscripts may or may not have contained.[331] So, assuming Yeshua really did say it, what does it mean? The English translation captures the Greek expression with one small deviation. The Greek doesn't say 'in the name' — it says, '*into* the name'.[332] The Hebrew translation of the Apostolic Writings renders it:

לְשֵׁם (*l'shem*)[333]

---

[329] Matthew 28:19-20a, emphasis mine. It's probably worth mentioning that, in his first letter to his young protégé Timothy, the Apostle Paul wrote:

*I charge you before **God** and the **Lord Jesus Christ** and the **elect angels** that you observe these things without prejudice, doing nothing with partiality. (1 Timothy 5:21 – emphasis mine).*

Are we to understand by this instruction that the 'elect angels' are also part of the trinity?

[330] Acts 2:38b.

[331] The church historian Eusebius of Caesarea claimed that Matthew was originally written in Hebrew, although there are no extant ancient copies to confirm this assertion. On the other hand, the trinitarian baptismal formula does appear in some early Christian writings — which may add weight to its inclusion in the original.

[332] εἰς τὸ ὄνομα (*eis to onoma*).

[333] הברית החדשה, (Israel Bible Society:Jerusalem 2000).

The preposition לְ (*l'*) is similar to the Greek equivalent, in that it implies 'in regard to' a location or goal. Whatever Yeshua meant by this expression, it was NOT intended as a verbal formula to accompany baptism. Nor does it make up a proof of the trinity.

Verses nineteen and twenty of Matthew chapter twenty-eight quoted above are the final verses in his gospel. The context is that Yeshua – Messiah the Son of Joseph – now raised from the dead, is commissioning his followers to take his message to others. He would return at some future time in his next role as Messiah the Son of David. As we have noted previously, there are quite a number of biblical messianic expectations still unfulfilled.

In this setting, Yeshua was describing a lifestyle for his followers that was to be characterised by the influence of God, the teachings of the Messiah, and the Spirit of God.

Now that We've Got that Sorted...

Some years ago, I was a member of a church that had a prison ministry. Every so often, a few of the guys would go to the local men's 'correctional facility' [334] and engage in discussions with the inmates on spiritual matters.[335] I recall one of the men involved in this pursuit telling the church that he'd had a number of conversations with a Muslim inmate. This gentleman had expressed his desire to become a Christian and

---

[334] PC for 'gaol'.

[335] Let's be truthful, they were proselytising – trying to make converts.

would have done so earlier, were it not for the doctrine of the Trinity. The would-be evangelist shared that he was unable to help this Muslim fellow any further because (the church member said):

"The Trinity is the foundation of our faith."

Is that true?

Unfortunately, to most Christians it is perfectly true, and any suggestion to the contrary is met with horror and righteous indignation at what is plainly heretical.

Fast-forward a number of years and I was having a conversation with a devout and well-educated Muslim lady in Saudi Arabia. When I explained my position on the Trinity, her response was:

"Well, that makes sense."

In this highly contentious section (especially to Christians), my aim is to present a similar argument to the one that I offered years ago in Riyadh, to see if anybody else out there – whether or not they agree with me – can see it as a preferable explanation of the ineffable God than the traditional Christian approach.

Chapter One:
What does God look Like?

No, I'm not being flippant. How would you describe God's appearance? If Michelangelo's Sistine Chapel ceiling is any guide, God is a distinguished-looking, bare-chested, older gentleman with a grey beard, flowing hair and an extended right index finger. In all fairness to Mikey the Chapel-Painter, I seriously doubt that he considered his artwork to be a genuine portrait of the Most High God – it was merely a representation and the reflection of a mediaeval imaginary construct.[336]

So, what does God really look like. Let's consider some theophanies (physical manifestations of God) as they appear in God's holy word. Again, we will take these texts at face value, rather than seeking deep and philosophical contrary explanations.

---

[336] Likewise, da Vinci's depiction of the Last Supper. Great painting, but it definitely earns a score of zero for historical accuracy. I mean, nice, leavened bread rolls at a Passover meal? Really? And that's just one of the many things wrong with it. Similarly, I was in Florence years ago and got to see his famous statue of David. Since he was a *Jewish* king, I noticed that there was something very wrong about the naked David's gentlemen's parts!

In the Torah

Strolling in the Garden

And they heard the sound of the LORD God walking in the garden in the cool of the day, and Adam and his wife hid themselves from the presence of the LORD God among the trees of the garden.[337]

Following their disobedience, Adam and Eve made a vain attempt to hide from their Creator, when they heard him 'walking'[338] in the garden. Whatever else may be deduced from this passage, we can at least determine that God didn't 'glide' or 'appear' – he was *walking*. Does that mean God has legs and feet (whatever they may look like?).

The Burning Bush[339]

The first time Moses met God, he was in the form of a burning bush. That this mysterious object was a manifestation of God, is implicit in the passage for, when Moses tries to approach the bush, God speaks to him:

Then He said, "Do not draw near this place. Take your sandals off your feet, for the place where you stand is holy ground." Moreover He said, "I am the God of your father—the God of Abraham, the God of Isaac, and the

---

[337] Genesis 3:8.

[338] Hebrew: מִתְהַלֵּךְ (mithaleik). This expression is the reflexive form of the verb *walk*. It means [kind of] 'causing himself to walk'. Presumably, God doesn't **have** to walk if he doesn't want to.

[339] Not the old 'Bull & Bush' – that's a pub.

God of Jacob." And Moses hid his face, for he was afraid to look upon God.[340]

The inevitable conclusion from this incident is that God can appear in a different *form*, if he chooses to do so.

The Shekinah

On their way to the Red Sea (and beyond) God manifested his presence to the people as the pillar of smoke or fire that they should follow:

> *And the LORD went before them by day in a pillar of cloud to lead the way, and by night in a pillar of fire to give them light, so as to go by day and night. He did not take away the pillar of cloud by day or the pillar of fire by night from before the people.*[341]

At Mount Sinai

God's arrival on the mountain was announced in a much more dramatic way than in the earlier examples:

> *Then it came to pass on the third day, in the morning, that there were thunderings and lightnings, and a thick cloud on the mountain; and the sound of the trumpet was very loud, so that all the people who were in the camp trembled.*[342]

---

[340] Exodus 3:5–6.

[341] Exodus 13:21–22.

[342] Exodus 19:16.

And when he arrived atop the mountain, he came once more in a fiery form:

Now Mount Sinai was completely in smoke, because the LORD descended upon it in fire.

Thus, God can also make a grand entrance if he chooses to do so.

After the Golden Calf

Moses' meeting with God took a little longer than the people anticipated. Inevitably, the people grew a bit restless and thought it would be a jolly fine idea to fashion a golden baby moo cow that they could worship.

Fail.

Moses, somewhat displeased with their conduct, ordered that the apostates be killed with the sword.[343] Subsequently, at the 'tent of meeting' the LORD would appear to Moses – in a familiar form:

And it came to pass, when Moses entered the tabernacle, that the pillar of cloud descended and stood at the door of the tabernacle, and the LORD talked with Moses.[344]

---

[343] Gently, of course.

[344] Exodus 33:9.

The Glory of God

Shortly after the above meeting and while he was plainly on a roll, Moses asked to see God's glory. The divine response is intriguing:

Then He said, "I will make all My goodness pass before you, and I will proclaim the name of the LORD before you..." But He said, "You cannot see My face; ***for no man shall see Me, and live.*** *" And the LORD said, "Here is a place by Me, and you shall stand on the rock. So it shall be, while My glory passes by, that I will put you in the cleft of the rock, and will cover you with My hand while I pass by. Then I will take away My hand, and you shall see My back; but My face shall not be seen. "* [345]

What's this all about? First, is God's reference to his hands, face and back simply an anthropomorphism [346] to aid Moses' understanding. Or does God have body parts? That is, when he's not being a bush or a pillar of cloud or fire or whatever else?

Is it true that seeing God's face results in lethal force? So it would seem. That was the reason for the high priest's use of incense at Yom Kippur:

And he shall put the incense on the fire before the LORD, that the cloud of incense may cover the mercy seat that is on the Testimony, lest he die. [347]

---

[345] Exodus 33:19–23, emphasis mine.

[346] A big word meaning 'assigning human form to something or someone who may not have human form'.

[347] Leviticus 16:13

The much maligned and misunderstood Apostle to the Gentiles, Paul, says something remarkably similar in the letter to his young protégé Timothy:

> *[God] alone has immortality, dwelling in unapproachable light, whom no man has seen or can see, to whom be honour and everlasting power. Amen.*[348]

But wait, there's more…

Aaron & Miriam's Dissent

Aaron and Miriam took umbrage with Moses' marriage to a Cushite woman and spoke against him in the Book of Numbers chapter twelve. God was displeased with their disloyalty to his appointed leader and took them to task, appearing in his pillar of cloud form:

> *Hear now My words: If there is a prophet among you,*
> *I, the LORD, make Myself known to him in a vision; I speak to him in a dream. Not so with My servant Moses; He is faithful in all My house.*[349]

So far, so good. But then the LORD, upon whose face nobody can look and survive continues:

> *I speak with him **face to face**, even plainly, and not in dark sayings; and he sees the form of the LORD.*[350]

---

[348] 1 Timothy 6:16.

[349] Numbers 12:6-7.

[350] Numbers 12:8a, emphasis mine. The expression פֶּה אֶל־פֶּה (peh–al–peh) is literally 'mouth-to-mouth', whatever that means.

Let's take stock for a moment. So far we've seen that God can appear in a variety of forms, but none may look upon his face in all its glory. Moses saw God's glory from behind and was able to see his 'form' when they spoke together.

Now, some of my Christian readers may be thinking that they know where I'm going with all this business of God being able to appear to men in **different forms**. You may be anticipating that, at some stage I will make a case for the unorthodox Christian doctrine professed by 'Oneness Pentecostalism'. In this denomination it is taught that there is one God (as per the *sh'ma*) but he can appear in different forms, to wit: the Father OR the Son OR the Holy Spirit.[351]

No, think again. That's a silly viewpoint.

In the Prophets

The above paragraphs notwithstanding, there are instances in the prophetic scriptures in which prophets encountered the LORD, in mind-blowing up-close and personal ways.

Isaiah

In the eighth century BCE, the prophet Isaiah saw God seated on his throne in the temple. His experience is recorded in the sixth chapter of the book bearing his name:

---

[351] Its technical name is 'modalism'.

In the year that King Uzziah died,[352] *I saw the Lord sitting on a throne, high and lifted up, and the train of His robe filled the temple.*[353]

The implications of seeing God in this way were not lost on the prophet, as he noted a few verses later:

So I said: "Woe is me, for I am undone! Because I am a man of unclean lips, and I dwell in the midst of a people of unclean lips; for my eyes have seen the King, the LORD of hosts."[354]

fortunately, Isaiah didn't suffer summary execution. Instead, a Seraph touched the hapless prophet's lips with a coal from the altar, thereby removing his sin. [355] Isaiah was summarily commissioned to his prophetic calling.[356]

Ezekiel

In a similar fashion to his predecessor, Ezekiel had a very strange encounter with the living God in the early sixth century BCE:[357]

And above the firmament over their heads was the likeness of a throne, in appearance like a sapphire stone; on the

---

[352] c.740 BCE.

[353] Isaiah 6:1.

[354] Isaiah 6:5.

[355] Isaiah 6:6-7.

[356] Isaiah 6:8-13.

[357] c.597 BCE.

likeness of the throne was a likeness with the appearance of a man high above it. Also from the appearance of His waist and upward I saw, as it were, the colour of amber with the appearance of fire all around within it; and from the appearance of His waist and downward I saw, as it were, the appearance of fire with brightness all around. Like the appearance of a rainbow in a cloud on a rainy day, so was the appearance of the brightness all around it. This was the appearance of the likeness of the glory of the LORD.[358]

If Ezekiel was overwhelmed in fear of his life, we are not told so in the biblical account.

So, What's the Bottom Line?

We've seen in this brief study of major theophanies in the Tanakh, that God appears to man in different forms of his choosing: burning bush; pillar of fire or smoke, or even enthroned in his heavenly temple. Additionally, we discovered that man cannot look God's face in all its glory and live. The fact that two of God's holy prophets looked upon his divine countenance (and lived to tell the tale) leads us to the conclusion that he can somehow diminish his glory at will, in the interests of human life preservation.

The bottom line is that precise definition of God's ontological nature is **beyond human comprehension**. Attempting to do so is akin to endeavouring to explain quantum physics to my border collie.[359]

---

[358] Ezekiel 1:26–28.

[359] Or, to me, for that matter.

And here's the thing…[360]

We haven't even considered God's 'angel' – whoever he may be. Perhaps it's time that we did.

---

[360] Now, *that's* a fine introduction for a 50s horror film, if ever I heard one.

Chapter Two:
The Angel of the LORD

Now that we that we are utterly nonplussed by the precise nature of our Creator – who surely exists outside of every dimension that string theorists[361] may determine there are – it's time to dig a little deeper.

There are occasions in holy writ where a mysterious individual, the Angel of the LORD, appears on the scene. This person comes across as wielding all the authority of God himself. Some Christian theologians, using exquisite circular logic, claim this person is actually the 'pre-incarnate' Christ. Sadly, there isn't a verse in either the Tanakh or the Apostolic Writings that they can use in support of this speculative theory.[362]

Let's look at a couple of instances – onwards and upwards…

The Torah

Hagar

This rather special angel makes his entry in Genesis sixteen, appearing to Hagar after her banishment at the hands of her

---

[361] You know, like your old violin tutor, when you were a kid.

[362] Some also suggest the same secret identity for the kingly priest Melchizedek (Genesis 14), and the Captain of the Host (Joshua 5).

mistress Sarai. Following significant prophetic details about Hagar's future, she gives her angelic visitor a name,[363] declaring that it was the LORD who spoke to her:

Then she called the name of the LORD who spoke to her, You-Are-the-God-Who-Sees; for she said, "Have I also here seen Him who sees me?"[364]

The question is, was this really God himself, in the form of a messenger,[365] or was the messenger acting as his envoy and thus bearing all of God's authority?

Abraham

Even more confusing is Abraham's interchange with God, a few chapters later in Genesis. I refer to the time when God tested him by commanding him to sacrifice his son Isaac. Initially, it is God who speaks to Abraham:

Now it came to pass after these things that God tested Abraham, and said to him, "Abraham!" And he said, "Here I am."[366]

Nevertheless, as Abraham demonstrates his willingness to obey the divine instruction, he is prevented from carrying out

---

[363] אֵל רָאִי (El Roi) the 'God who sees'. Not to be confused with 'Kilroy' who appears in various places.

[364] Genesis 16:13 – emphasis mine.

[365] Both the Hebrew and Greek words for 'angel' mean 'messenger'. In fact, the English word comes directly from the Greek: ἄγγελος (*angelos*).

[366] Genesis 22:1

his order by a voice from heaven. And this time it is the 'Angel of the LORD' who speaks to him:

But the Angel of the LORD called to him from heaven and said, "Abraham, Abraham!" So he said, "Here I am!" [367]

Adding to the confusion is, in the following verse, the Angel speaks in both the third **and** first person as God:

And He said, "Do not lay your hand on the lad, or do anything to him; for now I know that you fear God, since you have not withheld your son, your only son, from Me."
368

Weirder still, is Abraham's meeting with the LORD at Mamre. To begin with, his visitor is introduced as the LORD:

Then the LORD appeared to him by the terebinth trees of Mamre, as he was sitting in the tent door in the heat of the day. [369]

But when Abraham looks up, he sees three men standing by him, [370] whom he addresses in the singular term 'my Lord': [371]

---

[367] Genesis 22:11.

[368] Genesis 22:12 – also verses 15-18.

[369] Genesis 18:1.

[370] Trinitarians love this text!

[371] Noting that 'my Lord' in Hebrew is אֲדֹנָי (Adonai), the most popular circumlocution for the holy tetragrammaton. Thus, it could be a substitute for God his plural ending אֱלֹהִים (Elohim) or, perhaps it should be translated 'my lords' as it is in Genesis 19:2

So he lifted his eyes and looked, and behold, three men were standing by him; and when he saw them, he ran from the tent door to meet them, and bowed himself to the ground, and said, "My Lord, if I have now found favour in Your sight, do not pass on by Your servant. [372]

If the LORD can appear as a bush, an angel or a pillar of fire, is it too much to ask that he can appear in human form (or several human forms simultaneously), should he so desire?

Jacob and the Angel

Between Beersheba and Haran, Jacob dreamt of a ladder with angels ascending and descending upon it. Above this ladder stood the LORD himself. [373] Jacob named the place 'Bethel' [374] and placed a commemorative stone pillar at the site. A few chapters later, he receives instructions in a dream from the 'Angel of God', [375] who identifies himself as the very same LORD, whom Jacob encountered in his dream:

I am the God of Bethel, where you anointed the pillar and where you made a vow to Me. Now arise, get out of this land, and return to the land of your family. [376]

But wait, there's more!

---

[372] Genesis 18:2-3.

[373] Genesis 28:13.

[374] Hebrew בֵּיתְאֵל (*beitel*), meaning 'house of God'.

[375] Genesis 31:11.

[376] Genesis 31:13.

On his way home, Jacob engages in an all-night bout of 'no-holds-barred' wrestling with a very mysterious 'man', insisting that the latter bless him.[377] The 'man' renames him 'Israel'. All good but, this time Jacob designates the place 'Peniel',[378] on the basis that he has seen God 'face-to-face' and not been killed in the process[379] which, as we have seen in the case of Moses in the cleft of the rock, should have resulted in Jacob's certain death.

In the Book of Numbers this special 'angel' makes an appearance on the scene, but only to a donkey! The rent-a-prophet Balaam is blissfully unaware of his presence.[380]

The Former Prophets

Joshua

At the beginning of this chapter, I mentioned 'the Captain of the LORD's Host', in passing.[381] Let's now review the incident of Joshua's meeting with this unusual personage.

Nearing Jericho, Joshua espied a man with drawn sword,[382] who declared his identity as:

---

[377] Genesis 32:24–26.

[378] Hebrew פְּנִיאֵל (p'niel) meaning 'face of God'.

[379] Genesis 32:30.

[380] Once he realised his ignorance, it really sat him on his ass.

[381] See footnote 2.

[382] I suspect it was drawn in crayon on a pale pink cardboard background.

...Commander of the army of the LORD...[383]

Fine, Joshua has encountered an angelic warrior. So why did this 'messenger' with a military bearing[384] order Joshua to:

...Take your sandal off your foot, for the place where you stand is holy...[385]

the very same directive that Moses received from the LORD at the burning bush.[386]

As the Captain of the Host reveals to Joshua the proper tactics to take the fortified city of Jericho, he is again identified as God himself:

And the LORD said to Joshua: "See! I have given Jericho into your hand...[387]

Judges

The Angel appears in four chapters of the Book of Judges.[388] In chapter six, we find him sitting under a tree,[389]

---

[383] Joshua 5:14b. Hebrew שַׂר־צְבָא־יְהוָה (*sar-tsava-Adonai*), meaning 'prince of the LORD's army'.

[384] For the mechanically minded, a military bearing is nothing at all like a wheel bearing.

[385] Joshua 5:15b.

[386] By the way, Moses was ordered to remove his sandals by the one initially described as the 'Angel of the LORD' – Exodus 3:2.

[387] Joshua 6:2a.

[388] Judges chapters 2,5,6,13.

[389] Judges 6:11.

and holding a staff in his hand.[390] More interesting is the dialogue that takes place between him and Manoah, the father of Samson. Initially, Samson's mother describes him to her husband as a 'Man of God'.[391] Subsequently. he is simply referred to as 'the Man'.[392] In the rest of the chapter, he is identified as the 'Angel of the LORD',[393] but Manoah asks him what his name is in verse seventeen. The Angel opts not to reveal his name:

And the Angel of the LORD said to him, "Why do you ask My name, seeing it is wonderful?" [394]

However, his subsequent behaviour demonstrates that he is indeed God's angel.[395] Manoah and his wife then recognise that the Angel of the LORD is none other than the LORD himself, with the usual fear of repercussion surfacing, for having set eyes upon him:

And Manoah said to his wife, "We shall surely die, because we have seen God!" But his wife said to him, "If the LORD had desired to kill us, He would not have accepted a burnt offering and a grain offering from our hands... [396]

---

[390] Judges 6:21. I wonder if he was having a staff meeting?

[391] Judges 13:6. Manoah uses the same term in verse 8.

[392] Judges 13:10,11.

[393] Judges 13:13.

[394] Judges 13:18, Hebrew: פֶּלִאי *(peliy),* meaning 'incomprehensible, mysterious, wonderful'.

[395] Judges 13:20-21.

[396] Judges 13:22-23a.

2 Samuel

Following David's folly in taking out a census of Israel and Judah, God punished him by sending a three-day plague upon Israel, causing the deaths of seventy thousand men. When the angel wreaking all that devastation was about to visit destruction upon the people of Jerusalem, the LORD instructed the angel to desist.[397] The verse concludes as follows:

> *…And the angel of the LORD was by the threshing floor of Araunah the Jebusite.*[398]

If the angel who caused the plague is the same angel who was near Arahuah's threshing floor, then the LORD gave instructions to the Angel of the LORD.[399] As we've already seen, other texts maintain that they are one and the same person.

The Writings

Psalms

Further evidence that the LORD is equivalent to his angel can be found in Psalm thirty-four, which infers that the 'angel' can be present in a large area – unlike an individual:

---

[397] 2 Samuel 24:16a.

[398] 2 Samuel 24:16b.

[399] It was certainly the Angel of the LORD who killed 185,000 Assryians in 2 Kings 19:35 (also Isaiah 37:36).

The angel of the LORD encamps all around those who fear Him, and delivers them.[400]

The Twelve

Zechariah

One more example, just for grins, and then we'll wrap this chapter up. In the first chapter of the Book of Zechariah, the prophet sees four horses of different hues – the red one [at least] bearing a rider.[401] An angel explains to Zechariah that these horses have been sent throughout the earth by the LORD.[402] They report that all is quiet; the next verse showing that their account is given to the Angel of the LORD.[403]

The third chapter of Zechariah begins with Joshua the high priest being accused by Satan, in the presence of the Angel of the LORD. Initially, the LORD appears to respond:

And the LORD said to Satan, "The LORD rebuke you, Satan! The LORD who has chosen Jerusalem rebuke you! Is this not a brand plucked from the fire?" [404]

A little later, though, it is the Angel of the LORD, who continues to speak as God's agent or mouthpiece:

---

[400] Psalm 34:7.

[401] Who was probably of a different Hugh.

[402] Zechariah 1:10.

[403] Zechariah 1:11 – (also verse 12).

[404] Zechariah 3:2.

Then the Angel of the LORD admonished Joshua, saying, "Thus says the LORD of hosts: 'If you will walk in My ways, and if you will keep My command...[405]

So, What's the Bottom Line?

The most probable conclusion is that God can manifest himself into our world as a messenger – the Angel of the LORD – who takes a form similar to that of a man, simultaneously retaining his individuality.

Am I slyly setting my Jewish readers up for a trinitarian conclusion? Is this, after all one of those, "I come to bury Caesar, not to praise him" arguments?

Nope.

What I am saying is that God is utterly mysterious to us in our limited dimensional capacity. Any human endeavour to pin down God's exact nature – much as we might a new species of butterfly – is nothing short of folly. It's no different than trying to find an honest politician or infinitely split infinitives.

As I said previously, in the next section of this book I want to investigate the trinitarian claims of orthodox Christianity and try to come up with a better idea than Hellenistic trinitarianism – something instead with its roots in Jewish thought.

---

[405] Zechariah 3:6-7a.

Before that, though let's examine the Apostolic Writings for those texts used to prove that Yeshua boldly claimed that he was none other than God himself.

Chapter Three:
Because I said So...

As I've mentioned previously, most Christians see any attempt to undermine trinitarianism as being heretical-gusting-blasphemous. How is it that a dogma nowhere explicitly stated in either the Tanakh or Apostolic Writings can be so strenuously defended? In this chapter we will examine the deeply-cherished Christian belief that Yeshua is God because he declared himself to be so.

Yeshua's Attitude to the Trinity

Whatever else we discover in this chapter, it will be helpful to keep uppermost in our thoughts the words of Yeshua, as recorded in the gospel of Mark. The text recounts an incident where a scribe was impressed with Yeshua's reasoning:

Then one of the scribes came, and having heard them reasoning together, perceiving that He had answered them well, asked Him, "Which is the first commandment of all?" Jesus answered him, "The first of all the commandments is: 'Hear, O Israel, the LORD our God, the LORD is one. And you shall love the LORD your God with all your heart, with all your soul, with all your mind, and with all your strength.' This is the first commandment. And the second, like it, is this: 'You shall love your neighbor as yourself.' There is no other commandment greater than these." So the scribe said to Him, "Well said, Teacher. You have spoken the truth, for there is one God, and there is no other but He. And to love Him with all the heart, with all the understanding, with all the soul, and with all the strength, and to love one's neighbor as oneself, is more than all the whole burnt offerings and sacrifices." Now when Jesus saw that he answered wisely, He said to him, "You are not far from the kingdom of God." [406]

Yeshua awarded primacy to the *sh'ma* as the greatest of all commandments. This proves his personal commitment to Jewish monotheism. Let that be foremost in our minds as we critically examine the texts used by historical Christianity to prove the trinitarian nature of God.

The main Christian 'proof' of Yeshua's self-disclosure of his deity comes from the eighth chapter will come from the of Gospel of John. As you are aware there are four gospels, and each seeks to paint a different portrait of Yeshua: Matthew seeks to prove Yeshua's messiahship to his Jewish readers. Mark, writing primarily to gentiles, aims to depict him as the suffering servant; Luke emphasises (to his gentile benefactor Theophilus) the humanity of Yeshua.

John's gospel was composed late in the first century CE – long after the other three.[407] It is clear that the author of the fourth gospel, after decades of reflection, has set out to accomplish something different. He strives to present the

---

[406] Mark 12:28-24a.

[407] Matthew, Mark and Luke have a number of similarities in the historical data they discuss. Hence, they are known as the *synoptic gospels.*

transcendence of Yeshua. Yeshua's claims to deity are drawn mostly from within this gospel.

Did He Really Say That?

The first hit obtained, following my google search for: 'Did Jesus claim to be God?' was a column by Christian apologist Hank Hanegraaf on the Christianity.com website. He unswervingly points to the eighth chapter of John's gospel to prove that Yeshua is God. He writes:

In John 8:58 Jesus went so far as to use the very words by which God revealed Himself to Moses from the burning bush (Exodus 3:14). To the Jews this was the epitome of blasphemy, for they knew that in doing so Jesus was clearly claiming to be God.[408]

Hanegraaf is referring to the incident in which Yeshua professed to exist prior to his birth. He was responding to critics who declared that he was a demonised Samaritan.[409] Here's what the passage says:

Your father Abraham rejoiced to see My day, and he saw it and was glad." Then the Jews[410] *said to Him, "You are*

---

[408] Hank Hanegraaf, *Did Jesus Claim to be God?*, www.xtny.com (accessed 09 August 2023).

[409] John 8:48.

[410] Only in John's account, are Yeshua's protagonists referred to as 'Jews'. Given that both Yeshua and John himself were both Jews, this is a bit difficult to understand. Tragically, it provides ammunition for the supersessionists who claim that God is finished with Israel and the Christian church has now somehow mysteriously replaced literal Israel. Which begs the question, "If God's promises to Israel weren't meant to be taken literally, how can we trust anything else he says?" Be that as it may, a careful

not yet fifty years old, and have You seen Abraham?" Jesus said to them, "Most assuredly, I say to you, before Abraham was, I AM. "[411]

You will note that the translators of this verse have capitalised the expression 'I am'. They have done this to "prove" that Yeshua was taking the LORD's name as given to Moses in Exodus 3:14 below where the words are similarly capitalised in my English bible:

And God said to Moses, "I AM WHO I AM." And He said, "Thus you shall say to the children of Israel, 'I AM has sent me to you.'" [412]

Is the conclusion drawn from the comparison of these two texts a valid one?

G'day Moses, My Name's...

Before we take Hanegraaf's argument any further, we must investigate exactly how God introduced himself to Moses. Did he actually give his name as 'I am'?

Not exactly, no.

---

reading of John reveals that he uses the term (in a derogatory sense) only in respect of religious officials, members of the Sanhedrin, etc.

[411] John 8:58.

[412] Exodus 3:14.

The basic form of the verb 'to be' in biblical Hebrew[413] is הָיָה (*hayah*) and means 'come to pass, happen, become, exist'. The expression 'I am' in the Hebrew text of Exodus three is one word: אֶהְיֶה (*ehyeh*). It's what's known as a *qal imperfect* in the first person singular. The *qal* stem implies a verb in its simplest form. It expresses a simple action or status. However, the *imperfect* tense means that it is incomplete at the time of statement. This can indicate that the action hasn't yet happened – like the English future tense – or, as in this case in Exodus three, that it is an ongoing action.

In the first part of Exodus 3:14, where the English says, 'I AM who I AM, the Hebrew:

אֶהְיֶה אֲשֶׁר אֶהְיֶה (*ehyeh asher ehyeh*)

is really saying:
"I am the one who always exists, in that I am the one who always exists."

The Greek text of the Septuagint attempts to portray this concept with the **asymmetrical** expression:

Ἐγώ εἰμι ὁ ὤν.

This translates as:

"I am the existing [one]."

---

[413] In biblical Hebrew, the third person, masculine, singular *qal* [= light, simple'] perfect (already completed) is taken as the basic verbal form, e.g., '[he] ran'. In English, we tend to use the infinitive form 'to run' as the basic form of a verb. Hebrew also has infinitives but, they use the third person masculine singular *qal* perfect as the basic verb because... well... just because, okay?

God introduced himself to Moses as the one who has existed, now exists, and will continue to exist forever. In the second part of the Exodus verse, God truncates his divine epithet:

"Thus you shall say to the children of Israel, 'I AM has sent me to you.'"
to the first word only of his three-term appellation. In Hebrew:

אֶהְיֶה (ehyeh)

The English 'I AM' captures the intent of God's abbreviation to some degree. However, consider this made-up verse from the non-existent Gospel of Barry:

Then Mavis asked, "Who's going to nip up the road and buy us all some hot chips?" Graham replied, "I am."

This could hardly be touted as a proof of Graham's belief in his own divinity.

Do you Speaka My Language?

The other difficulty with Hanegraaf's traditional argument is that the Apostolic Writings were composed in Greek, whereas the Tanakh was written in Hebrew. So what language was Yeshua speaking when he said the words attributed to him in the Gospel of John?

It is highly unlikely that he was conversing in Greek. For quite some time it was taught that Yeshua spoke Aramaic — even that highly regarded biblical scholar Mel Gibson said so.[414] Nonetheless, recent research has suggested that Hebrew may have been more widely spoken in ancient Judea than was previously thought[415] And, in Yeshua's case, there is a pericope in which he conversed easily with a Samaritan woman.[416] The Samaritans, having assimilated with their Assyrian victors, predated Judah's exile to Babylon and preserved the Hebrew tongue in the process.

My point is that John **translated** Yeshua's words into Greek when he compiled his gospel. The Greek words he chose for Yeshua's response to his adversaries:

...*before Abraham was, I AM,*

is the clause:

πρὶν Ἀβραὰμ γενέσθαι ἐγὼ εἰμί. (*prin Abra'am genesthai ego eimi.*)

which translates as:

before Abraham came into being, I am.

The expression 'I am' (*ego eimi*) – the first two words of the Septuagint translation of God's longer moniker – is in the Greek present tense which, unlike English, is a continuous tense. That is to say that it implies an ongoing status.

---

[414] I refer, of course, to his movie *The Passion,* in which the cast members were required to learn their lines in Aramaic.

[415] For instance, the Dead Sea Scrolls were mostly written in Hebrew.

[416] John 4:1–26.

Whichever way we look at it, Yeshua is making a statement that he existed, in some manner, prior to Abraham. Whether he was delusional or making a true statement is not the point. The point is that this text should ***not*** be used to 'prove' that Yeshua claimed to be God.

IF Yeshua uttered those exact words ***in Gre***ek.

It is highly likely that he was actually speaking Hebrew (or Aramaic). If so, what were his exact words?

We simply don't know.

It is unlikely that he said the words, 'I am', for there is no direct Hebrew equivalent for this expression.[417]

So What's the Bottom Line?

The bottom line is that Yeshua was committed to Jewish monotheism, proven by his insistence that the greatest commandment of all was the *sh'ma*. In the eighth chapter of the gospel of John, he asserted his own existence prior to Abraham (who lived around two millennia before him), according to the Greek translation of his words. Whatever he meant by that[418] it isn't the same thing as saying, "Look here, you lot, you better shape up because I'm God!"

---

[417] The verb 'to be' is implicit in Hebrew in the present tense, not spoken. Thus, a policeman stating his occupation would say אֲנִי שׁוֹטֵר *(ani shoter)*, literally: 'I policeman'.

[418] I cited this text in Part Three as supporting Second Temple Jewish belief in the pre-existence of Messiah, as revealed in the Intertestamental Literature. But to say that I existed before King Henry VIII (whether I'm crazy or not) is not the same thing as saying that I'm God.

So, if Yeshua didn't actually say he was God, he must have implied somehow in his words or actions, right?

Let's see...

Chapter Four:
Just Read Between the Lines, Guys...

We noted in the previous chapter that, although Yeshua made a seemingly bizarre statement that he existed prior to the great Patriarch Abraham, nowhere in the Apostolic Writings did he directly claim to be God. In this chapter we will consider the Christian assertions for the deity of Yeshua based on his words by which, it is said, he implied his divinity.

Who's your Daddy?

There are two more instances in John's narrative that Christians use to prove that Yeshua indirectly declared himself to be God. In the first example, Yeshua referred to God as his 'Father'. His words, according to John were:

My Father has been working until now, and I have been working.[419]

This upset his enemies, who accused him of blasphemy because, according to the next verse of the passage:

...[Yeshua] said that God was His Father, making Himself equal with God.[420]

---

[419] John 5:17b.

[420] John 5:18b.

This is somewhat perplexing.

King David blessed the LORD before the whole assembly as follows:

*Blessed are You, LORD God of Israel, **our Father**, forever and ever.*[421]

Given that Jews have been referring to God as their father for *at least* the last three thousand years,[422] it is difficult to understand why Yeshua's opponents expressed such anger at his words. Perhaps it was his use of the personal pronoun 'my' – did that suggest some sort of exclusivity?

I am Unanimous in This...

The second incident in John's account occurs in the tenth chapter. Here Yeshua makes the statement:

I and My Father are one.[423]

In context, Yeshua is again referring to God as his 'Father', to which his enemies took offence, picking up stones to stone him. Yeshua responded:

---

[421] 1 Chronicles 29:10b, emphasis mine.

[422] See Deuteronomy 32:6 for an example in the Torah. Other examples from the Tanakh include Isaiah 63:16; 64:8; Jeremiah 31:9; Hosea 1:10; 11:1 (by inference), and Malachi 2:10. The concept of God as the father of Israel is similarly found in non-canonical texts: Wisdom, Tobit, Sirach and the Dead Sea Scrolls. An ancient Jewish prayer begins *(Avinu Malkeinu)* – 'Our Father, Our King' and the fourth and fifth benedictions in the *Amidah* refer to God as 'our father'.

[423] John 10:30.

"Many good works I have shown you from My Father. For which of those works do you stone Me?" The Jews answered Him, saying, "For a good work we do not stone You, but for blasphemy, and because You, being a Man, make Yourself God." [424]

Let us assume that their accusation was valid and that Yeshua was indeed claiming to be God. This was his opportunity to make his position clear. He could have responded along the lines of:

Yes, I certainly am God and thou'd better put those rocks down before I smiteth thee!

Instead, Yeshua quoted the Tanakh, while reinforcing his belief in his filial relationship to God:

Jesus answered them, "Is it not written in your law, 'I said, "You are gods"'? If He called them gods, to whom the word of God came (and the Scripture cannot be broken), do you say of Him whom the Father sanctified and sent into the world, 'You are blaspheming,' because I said, 'I am the Son of God

Two questions need to be addressed here: What precisely did he mean by the statements: *'I and my father are one'* and *'I am the son of God'?* [425]

---

[424] John 10:32–33.

[425] John 10:34–36, Yeshua is quoting Psalm 82:6.

Son of God?

Let's try and answer the second one first.[426] The term 'son of God' was nothing new to the era of Second Temple Judaism. It was a name often adopted by kings. For example, the infamous, and indisputably deranged, first-century CE Roman Emperor adopted the title *Nero Divi Filius* – Nero, the son of god.

Moreover, the second Psalm, sung at coronations, clearly refers to the King of Israel as God's son:

"Yet I have set My King on My holy hill of Zion." I will declare the decree: the LORD has said to Me 'You are My Son, today I have begotten You." [427]

In referring to God as his Father, it is more probably that Yeshua was making the audacious claim that he was the King of Israel i.e., he was proclaiming himself as Messiah.

I and My Father are One

Ironically, Christian expositors like to interpret Yeshua's statement here in the light of the *sh'ma.* If the LORD is 'one' and Yeshua and God are also 'one', it follows that Yeshua is God, or so the logic goes. Again, we have no way of knowing precisely what Yeshua's words were in Hebrew or Aramaic – we only have the Greek translation, which appears like this:

---

[426] It sounds better if you pronounce the word 'first' as 'foist' *à la* Groucho Marx. Trust me on this.

[427] Psalm 2:6-7.

ἐγὼ καὶ ὁ πατὴρ ἕν ἐσμεν (*ego kai ho pate̱r hen esmen*)

Of significance in this Greek expression – noting that Yeshua wasn't speaking Greek – is that the word for 'one' (*hen*) is neuter in gender.[428] If Yeshua was declaring that he and his father were the **one person**, the masculine form of 'one' εἷς (heis) would have been more appropriate.[429] It is more likely that, based on the Greek (for what that's worth), he was proclaiming that he and God were of, for example, **one purpose**.

So What's the Bottom Line?

John, in his narrative, is trying to portray Yeshua as transcendent – that is, being more than just your average Joe. To do this, he has focussed on the more extraordinary claims that Yeshua made. In the previous chapter, we saw that Yeshua avowed his pre-existence. In this chapter, he has cryptically declared himself as the King of Israel, with a unity of purpose with God himself.

Strange words indeed, but not ironclad proof of his self-representation as God. A little later on, we will take another look at some of John's gospel which, I hope, will give us a better insight into Yeshua's strange statements.

---

[428] Hebrew has only masculine and feminine gender; Greek also has the neuter.

[429] If you're wondering what the feminine Greek for 'one' is, it's μία *(mia)*, which proves that the Swedish pop group ABBA had only one mother.

Chapter Five:
What Will my Friends Say?

We have considered the words attributed to Yeshua in John's narrative, in the last two chapters. In this one we will examine the words of those who wrote about him in the remainder of the Apostolic Writings. Again, we will explore those texts which appear to support the contention that Yeshua is God.

Paul... Plus One?

There are half a dozen references implying the deity of Yeshua in the writings of the Apostle Paul. One of them is in the Letter to the Hebrews, written to Jewish followers of Yeshua dwelling in and around Jerusalem, prior to the destruction of the Temple in 70 CE. The fourth-century CE church historian, Eusebius of Caesarea, attributed this letter to Paul. However, later scholarship suggests that the writer was a 'different-other-chappie'. Maybe it was one of Paul's friends, like Barnabas... or perhaps it was Apollos... on the other hand it might have been... I dunno, somebody else.[430]

---

[430] The arguments against Pauline authorship are, in my opinion, less than convincing. Two quick examples for your consideration: First (it is said), the Greek in Hebrews differs in style to the Greek in other letters by Paul. My response is, "Well d'uh..." Eusebius (mentioned previously) noted 1700 years ago that the letter was originally written in Hebrew and later translated into Greek – by Luke, the author of the third gospel. Second, the letter to the Hebrews does not follow the Greco-Roman letter-writing protocols embraced by Paul in his letters to assemblies in the diaspora. Once again, the response must be, "no kiddin'?" Paul followed the Greek

Paul's Pointers

The following texts, taken from Paul's letters which, as we have seen earlier, were halachic instructions to the predominately gentile assemblies in the diaspora. We will examine them in order of their appearance in the Apostolic Writings.

To the Assembly at Corinth...

In his second letter to this group, Paul describes:

*...the glory of Christ, who is the **image of God**...*[431]

Since all mankind is created in the *imago dei,* it would be simple to ignore this statement as somewhat irrelevant. But, as the other Pauline texts we will view show, the Apostle to the Gentiles had something more in mind.

To the Assembly at Philippi...

This verse is more difficult to dismiss than the previous example:

*Let this mind be in you which was also in Christ Jesus, who, being **in the form of God**, did not consider it robbery*

---

letter-writing conventions when he wrote to Greeks. He dispensed with them when writing to Jews. Not exactly rocket science, is it? But wait, there's more! In Paul's letter to the Romans, he quotes Deuteronomy 32:5 in a composite form: partly the Hebrew wording and partly the Septuagint wording. The author of Hebrews makes precisely the same quote in his letter.

[431] 2 Corinthians 4:4b, emphasis mine.

to be equal with God, but made Himself of no reputation, taking the form of a bondservant, and coming in the likeness of men.[432]

This passage implies that Yeshua existed in some other form, before making his appearance on planet earth as a human being. What's more, Paul states that Yeshua was 'in the form of God'.

What does he mean by that?

The next two verses reinforce Yeshua's apparent 'change of form' into that of a man. But, at the same time, Paul maintains the distinction between Yeshua and God:

And being found in appearance as a man, He humbled Himself and became obedient to the point of death, even the death of the cross. Therefore God also has highly exalted Him and given Him the name which is above every name...[433]

The lynchpin for the Philippian passage is the in the expression I emphasised in the first text above:

...in the form of God.[434]

How are we to understand the phrase? Let's do the Geek of Greek thingy:

---

[432] Philippians 2:5-7, emphasis mine.

[433] Philippians 2:8-9.

[434] Philippians 2:6b.

...ἐν μορφῇ θεοῦ (en morphe theou)

To begin with, the definite article ('the') does not appear in the original text – it has been added by the English translators. Greek (like Hebrew) has no indefinite article (a, an) and should be supplied, where appropriate, to render a text into correct English. In this case, it is required and the English translation should read:

...in a form of God.

Hold that thought – we shall return to it.

To the Assembly at Colossae...

The Colossian passage begins like that to the Corinthians:

He is the image of the invisible God...[435]
and, had it stopped there, could be disregarded, as yet another statement of Yeshua's humanity. However, the text continues in a strange manner:

...the firstborn over all creation. For by Him all things were created that are in heaven and that are on earth, visible and invisible, whether thrones or dominions or principalities or powers. All things were created through Him and for Him.[436]

Now that's really 'out there'...

---

[435] Colossians 1:15a.

[436] Colossians 1:15b–16.

How could Yeshua be the 'firstborn over all creation' and the means and meaning of all created things?

To the Jews in Jerusalem...

The purpose of the Letter to the Hebrews in the Apostolic Writings was to encourage Jewish followers of Yeshua to 'hold the line', as it were, despite becoming increasingly disenfranchised by mainstream Judaism. As such he wastes no time in extolling Yeshua as a prominent figure in the greater scheme of things, as the first three verses reveal:

> *God, who at various times and in various ways spoke in time past to the fathers by the prophets, has in these last days spoken to us by His Son, whom He has appointed heir of all things, through whom also He made the worlds; who being the brightness of His glory and the express image of His person, and upholding all things by the word of His power, when He had by Himself purged our sins, sat down at the right hand of the Majesty on high, having become so much better than the angels, as He has by inheritance obtained a more excellent name than they.*[437]

In this passage, the writer has declared Yeshua to be the 'glory' and 'express image of God', through whom he 'made the world'.

The author of Hebrews, even if it wasn't Paul, was a Jew who was thoroughly familiar with the Tanakh and the Temple worship system of that era. Either he was rejecting Jewish monotheism in favour of (at least) a binary form of God, or we

---

[437] Hebrews 1:1-4.

must seek an alternative explanation for his grandiloquent language.

So What's the Bottom Line?

Whatever explanation we give to statements and inferences attributed to Yeshua himself by the gospel authors - John in particular — it is exceedingly difficult to make sense of the words penned by the Apostle Paul and the writer of the letter to the Hebrews (whoever that may have been).

There is an alternative, though, to the traditional Christian doctrine of the trinity. As I keep threatening to, we will investigate this other possibility in the next part of this book. But, before we go there, we haven't addressed the alleged third person of the Christian trinity: the Holy Spirit.

Next chapter, we will do so.

Chapter Six:
That's the Spirit!

We have addressed the more common proof texts for the divinity of Yeshua in the last few chapters. The third member of the Christian trinity has thus far avoided scrutiny and I refer to the Holy Spirit, of course.

For consistency, I once more quote from the Christianity.com website. The article was written by Alyssa Roat:

> The Holy Spirit is often misunderstood. Is the Holy Spirit an "it"? A "He"? Is the Holy Spirit a mystical energy, like "the force" in the Star Wars franchise? Or is it just another name for God? The Holy Spirit is God, a Person, not an energy or a force, just as much as the other two members of the Trinity.[438]

Unlike the quote from Hanegraaff that we saw in chapter one of this section, supporting the deity of Yeshua, Roat doesn't really offer anything in the way of scriptural support. Instead, she resorts to some historic Christian creeds as a substitute.

Having said that, the usual Christian defence of the Holy Spirit as both person and God is centred around a few texts which seem to imply both conditions.

---

[438] Roat, Alyssa, *www.christianity.com* (accessed 22 August 2023).

Let's examine them...

The Holy Spirit is God

The only 'proof text' worthy of consideration is found in the Apostolic Writings in the Book of Acts. The context is when the burgeoning body of Yeshua's Jewish followers were pooling their resources to establish a sort of commune lifestyle. An individual named Ananias pledged the receipts from a block of land that he'd sold, but deceitfully kept some of the takings for himself. The issue at stake was not that he kept some of his own funds back (as the text demonstrates), but that he'd allowed deception to infiltrate the group. The Apostle Peter discerned his duplicity and publicly called him out:

> *But Peter said, "Ananias, why has Satan filled your heart to* **lie to the Holy Spirit** *and keep back part of the price of the land for yourself? While it remained, was it not your own? And after it was sold, was it not in your own control? Why have you conceived this thing in your heart?* **You have not lied to men but to God.**"*[439]

The reasoning goes that Ananias lied to the Holy Spirit. Peter accused him of lying to God. Therefore, the Holy Spirit is God. That conclusion, while not entirely mistaken, is certainly incomplete.

More on that shortly...

---

[439] Acts 5:3-5 – emphasis mine.

The Holy Spirit is a Person

There are occasions in both the Tanakh and the Apostolic Writings in which the qualities of personhood are applied to the Holy Spirit. Here's a couple of examples from the Tanakh:

Then the Spirit entered me when He spoke to me, and set me on my feet; and I heard Him who spoke to me.[440]

But they rebelled and grieved His Holy Spirit; so He turned Himself against them as an enemy, and He fought against them.[441]

The [Holy] Spirit **spoke** to Ezekiel and, it is argued, only a sentient person can speak.[442] Moreover, Isaiah recalls how the past rebellion of his people had grieved the Holy Spirit. The reasoning goes, that a vague cosmic force or an 'it' does not have the qualities of personhood such as speech or emotions. Thus, the Holy Spirit must be a sentient being in his own right.

Are these Conclusions Valid?

Yes. That's the end of the book *[just kidding]*.

Let's take the second one first.[443]

---

[440] Ezekiel 2:2 – by 'person' we probably have to include Balaam's donkey who was temporarily and supernaturally given the opportunity to input her tuppence worth (Numbers 22:28–30).

[441] Isaiah 63:10.

[443] Recall that this word is to be pronounced: 'foist'. Thank you.

The peoples of ancient times were sometimes given to anthropomorphic speech. That is to say, personal qualities were projected onto created things that, ordinarily, wouldn't have these attributes.

Consider the following texts from the Tanakh:

For you shall go out with joy, and be led out with peace; The mountains and the hills shall break forth into singing before you, and all the trees of the field shall clap their hands.[444]

This is clearly poetry – nobody believes that hills can literally sing or that trees possess the ability to applause. And while this may be a straw man argument, it serves to remind us that, while everything in the bible is true, not everything is meant to be taken literally.[445] There *are* figures of speech in the sacred text.[446] Not only that, but sometimes personality is assigned to abstract concepts, such as 'wisdom':

Say to wisdom, "You are my sister," and call understanding your nearest kin,[447]

Does not wisdom cry out, and understanding lift up her voice? She takes her stand on the top of the high hill, beside the way, where the paths meet. She cries out by the

---

[444] Isaiah 55:10.

[445] Does God literally have wings and feathers (Psalm 91:4), for example?

[446] I recall reading somewhere that there are over two hundred different kinds of figures of speech in the bible. Not sure where that was… perhaps it was the *National Enquirer?*

[447] Proverbs 7:4.

gates, at the entry of the city, at the entrance of the doors: "To you, O men, I call, and my voice is to the sons of men. "[448]

Based on the two texts above, it would not be unreasonable to deduce that wisdom was, in truth, a person of the female persuasion.[449]

There is a verse in the Apostolic Writings (again in the gospel of John) in which the Holy Spirit is assigned a masculine pronoun, implying 'male' personhood. The English translations reflect the Christian belief in the deity of the Spirit by capitalising the words 'Helper' and 'He'. The context is this: Yeshua, knowing that his death was approaching, encouraged his disciples by assuring them of the presence of the Holy Spirit in their lives, to teach them, and to assist them in recalling his teachings, following his departure:

These things I have spoken to you while being present with you. But the Helper, the Holy Spirit, whom the Father will send in My name, He will teach you all things, and bring to your remembrance all things that I said to you.[450]

This appears to be a convincing argument because the Greek word translated 'He' is indeed the nominative masculine singular demonstrative pronoun ἐκεῖνος *(ekeinos)*. Once more, acknowledging that Yeshua probably wasn't speaking Greek at the time, that language (unlike Hebrew) does have a neuter

---

[448] Proverbs 8:1-4.

[449] In today's bizarre culture, that's plainly okay, because I can identify as a dark green will o' the wisp with fins, should I choose to do so. It's my right, okay?

[450] John 14:25-26.

gender and the Apostle could have chosen the Greek equivalent of 'it', rather than 'he' in writing down his narrative.

Is this game, set and match in favour of the personhood of the Holy Spirit?

Not entirely, no.

Consider this verse from the gospel of Matthew. Yeshua is speaking in this quote:

And he who does not take his cross and follow after Me is not worthy of Me. He who finds his life will lose it, and he who loses his life for My sake will find it.[451]

Germane to our study is this part of the couplet:

...find life... lose it; lose life... find it

specifically, we want to examine the repeated words 'life' and 'it'.

The word translated as 'life' is the Greek term ψυχὴν *(psuchen)*,[452] which is more accurately translated as 'soul'. The Greek language, as mentioned above, has all three genders.[453] Because the word *psuchen* is feminine in gender, in order to make the rest of the sentence grammatically correct in Greek, the word translated 'it' – αὐτήν *(auten)* – is also feminine in

---

[451] Matthew 10:38-39.

[452] It's the noun ψυχή *(psuche)* in its accusative feminine form. It's where English words like 'psychology' come from.

[453] An insufficient number of genders for today's woke world, obviously.

gender.[454] If we really wanted pinpoint precision we could translate *aute* as 'her' despite the awkwardness of the English that causes.

You can see where I'm going with this, can't you?

What is the gender of the noun which the pronoun in John's gospel relates to?
But the Helper, the Holy Spirit, whom the Father will send in My name, He will teach you all things...[455]

It is plainly the word 'Helper'. The Greek term 'helper' is παράκλητος *(parakletos)* and means 'one called beside' in the sense of an advocate, counsellor, or encourager. Now, to be honest, Yeshua's words do ***imply*** personhood for the *parakletos*. But it's not as ironclad a proof as is touted by Christians. The masculine *ekeinos* (he) simply agrees with the masculine *parakletos*. And if Yeshua was speaking metaphorically of the Spirit, it really boils down to whether the 'helper' is literally a person or not.

So, What's the Bottom Line?

The bottom line is simply that the biblical evidence for the Christian doctrine of the trinity is less than overwhelming. Then again, empty criticism is not a particularly skilful art.

Do I have a better explanation?

---

[454] See how the last couple of letters are the same? It's the feminine, accusative, third person, personal pronoun for those who are interested in such things. If that describes you, you probably have no real life to speak of.

[455] John 14:26a.

I hope so and that, as I have said throughout this chapter, is what the next section of this book is hopefully all about.

Part Five:
A Different Perspective

As I indicated in the previous section, there is an alternative view of the nature of God, which I shall present in this section, and it's easier to get one's brain around, than classical Christian trinitarian thought. It strives to preserve the monotheism of the *Sh'ma* while accommodating some of the more perplexing texts found within the Apostolic Writings.

At least I hope it does.

Something as beyond our grasp as the ontological nature of God is bound to require a lot of investigation and the establishment of some foundational ideas. That's a nice way of saying that I'm going to have to blather on quite a bit before I can finally present my case for this difficult issue. I crave your indulgence for that.

And while it still doesn't tear down the infrangible barrier between Jews and Christians (whom I will surely upset the most and risk the heretic's fate of burning) in this final segment of the book, I believe it is an easier position for both groups to begrudgingly accept.

You be the judge please...

Chapter One:
What is Man?

It seems a bit odd to ask that question in a section about the true nature of God but, bear with me if you will.[456] If we look at the makeup of man,[457] it may aid in our understanding of him who created us. And, at this stage in our journey together, it should come as no surprise that the Greek view of man differs from its Hebraic counterpart.

Greeksman

Greek-thinking Christian theologians have differing opinions on the nature of human beings. Some hold to the dichotomous view – man is comprised of two parts; others prefer the trichotomous view – there are three parts to man. The latter standpoint was common in the Greco-Roman world, through the influence of the great philosopher Plato.[458]

---

[456] As a streaker at a cricket match was heard to say to his friend.

[457] Yes, men do have the right to wear makeup today!

[458] Of whom some say, '… could put it away; half a crate of whisky every day.'

Dichotomous Man[459]

In the dichotomous camp, man is made up of two components: the physical and the non-physical. When the scriptures refer to the 'soul' of man:

My soul also is greatly troubled...[460]

or to the spirit of man:

But there is a spirit in man...[461]

these two terms are interchangeable and refer to the non-corporeal part of man that cannot be discerned with the physical senses.

Trichotomous Man[462]

The trichotomous opinion sees the 'soul' and 'spirit' as different non-physical parts of man. This view can be supported from a text within the Apostolic Writings. The Apostle Paul, writing to a predominantly gentile assembly in Thessalonica concluded his letter with a benediction:

*Now may the God of peace Himself sanctify you completely; and may your whole **spirit**, **soul**, and **body** be*

---

[459] No relation to Piltdown Man.

[460] Psalm 6:3a.

[461] Proverbs 32:8a.

[462] And, if you don't want to trichotomous man, you can try cottage cheese instead (but don't mix it with the meat!).

preserved blameless at the coming of our Lord Jesus Christ.[463]

In his use of the terms: 'body', 'soul' and 'spirit' it is possible that Paul was merely accommodating the Hellenistic understanding of his gentile readers. But regardless, the verse above does supply the perfect proof text for the trichotomous opinion.

What is the difference between the 'soul' and the 'spirit' according to this perspective? Most proponents see the 'soul' as also encompassing three parts: the 'mind', the 'will' and the 'emotion' – in other words, the personality of the individual – what they think, want and feel. That being the case, what is the 'spirit' of man?

Good question.

If the soul's function is to define our personality – how we relate to others and different situations - the spirit must have a 'higher' function. It is often taught that the spirit is the innermost part of man through which he relates to God and that it cannot really be discerned or described. Trichotomous thought holds an advantage over its dichotomous counterpart insofar as it benefits trinitarian thought. If man is made up of three parts and man is made in the image of God, then surely God is…

---

[463] 1 Thessalonians 5:23 – emphasis mine.

Hebrewsman

The Hebrew-thinker rejects the dichotomous versus trichotomous argument as being largely irrelevant. And let me ask you, dear reader, does it actually make a difference to *your* life, knowing whether the part of you that we can't see is a unit or a pair? Instead, the Hebraic view of man is derived from creation of Adam in the biblical narrative:

> *And the LORD God formed man of the dust of the ground, and breathed into his nostrils the breath of life; and man became a living being.*[464]

It will helpful to explore further three of the terms that appear in the original Hebrew of the above verse:

1. 'Breathed' is the Hebrew word נָפַח (*naphach*), meaning 'breathe' or 'blow' as in a movement of air.

2. 'Being' is נֶפֶשׁ (*nephesh*), a cognate of the previous word, often translated as 'soul'.

3. 'Breath' is נְשָׁמָה (*n'shamah*), which also means breath, as in a movement of air, especially when it comes from God.

How do these three terms relate to one another? Permit me to introduce yet another Hebrew term – רוּחַ (*ruach*), which means 'breath', 'wind' or 'spirit'.

---

[464] Genesis 2:7

Glassblower Man

There was once a Jewish sage – it *may* have been Rambam[465] – who conceived the glassblower analogy of the creation of man that we just looked at. A glassblower conceives and fashions his glass utensil from a formless lump by the force of his breath and skilful creativity.

Let's take his parallel a step further. Try this for size…

God, the master craftsman, breathes (*naphach*) down the glass tube. The power of his divine breath (*n'shamah*), his life-force, flows towards his creation to be. The power or motive force of his breath as it expands the hot glass shape is his spirit or wind (*ruach*). The man becomes a living soul (*nephesh*) through the breath of almighty God. As long as the man stays 'connected' to his creator by the divine *ruach* – he can be moulded and shaped to become more like the image of his creator. Once the glassblower is disconnected – in this case the man's decision instead of God's – the hollow and fragile glass shell remains. That is, until its lifespan is completed and it shatters against the irresistible force of mortality.

How many parts does the object being shaped possess? It really only had the one part; it is neither dichotomous nor trichotomous. The immaterial part (or parts), which God supplies, determines both the external shape and function of the utensil.

---

[465] I can't recall for sure who it was. If you're unfamiliar with the name 'Rambam', it is the affectionate name given to a great Jewish thinker, **R**abbi **M**oses **b**en **M**aimonides (1138-1204), based on the initials italicised. Get it?

From the Hebraic perspective, every living creature has a soul (*nephesh*). [466] Torah declares members of the animal kingdom to possess 'life' — but the word in bold in the text below is literally 'breath' or 'soul' (*nephesh*). This is demonstrated by the fact that they breathe (*naphach*).[467]

> *Also, to every beast of the earth, to every bird of the air, and to everything that creeps on the earth, in which there is **life**, I have given every green herb for food; and it was so.*[468]

What, if anything, sets humankind apart from other physical living creatures?

To be truthful, it's hard to say. In the flood narrative, both men and beasts are said to have *n'shamah:*

> *And all flesh died that moved on the earth: birds and cattle and beasts and every creeping thing that creeps on the earth, and every man. All in whose nostrils was the **breath of the spirit** of life, all that was on the dry land, died.*[469]

The phrase highlighted above, is the Hebrew: נִשְׁמַת־רוּחַ (*nishmat-ruach*). These are two of the words we've discussed

---

[466] No, sorry, the ancients weren't interested in bacteria or other non-visible creatures.

[467] In the absence of machines to monitor brain activity, breathing was the simple test of whether one was alive or dead.

[468] Genesis 1:30 — emphasis mine.

[469] Genesis 7:21-22 — emphasis mine cp. Genesis 6:17:

> *And behold, I Myself am bringing floodwaters on the earth, to destroy from under heaven all flesh in which is the breath of life; everything that is on the earth shall die.*

earlier in describing the creation of man. The first is simply a construct form of *n'shamah* (breath, especially originating from God) and the second is *ruach* meaning breath, spirit or wind.

The only difference that I can determine between humankind and the animal kingdom is – and this is just my opinion, mind you[470] - is that we are given no scriptural evidence that God personally breathed his *n'shamah* into any other life form than man. That's why we were uniquely created in the image of God, with the capacity for higher thought, deeper emotion and even lofty notions which may be foreign to other species, like self-sacrificial love.

So, What's the Bottom Line?

I guess we haven't really solved the precise nature of man's makeup and d'you know what? I'm okay with that.

Because, if nothing else, we are very complex beings.

Science still hasn't fully plumbed the depths of the physical organism, let alone that part of us which is the invisible 'ghost in the machine'.[471]

What does this have to do with God?

There is only one of me; there is only one of you. We are not comprised of independent segments – not really – whether

---

[470] Hey, I'm the author, it's my prerogative to give opinions, okay?

[471] Which is a little surprising because scientists know everything else about how we got to be here – just ask them.

we're bipartite, tripartite or poly-partite.[472] If we can't fully grasp what constitutes ourselves, what makes us think we can dissect and categorise the most high God?

Nonetheless, let's give it a whirl, shall we?

---

[472] Coincidentally, that's the name of a former neighbour of mine's parrot. A Norwegian Blue, as I recall.

Chapter Two:
The Spirit of God

What is the precise nature of God? Given that we struggle to define the nature of man, the honest answer has to be that we simply don't have foggiest notion. And any attempt to come up with something tangible is fraught with peril as we are treading on sacred ground.[473] But, if that's all there is to it, this would be, of necessity, a very short chapter. Besides, if you were silly enough to pay for this book, you have the right to expect some kind of explanation herein. Let's attempt to expand our tiny capabilities together, as best we can.

As we do so, let us uphold the tradition that the terms 'Spirit of God', 'Spirit of the LORD' and 'Holy Spirit' are synonyms.

Here goes…

In the Beginning…

We are introduced to God quite early in the scriptural narrative. In fact, the introduction takes place in the very first verse:

In the beginning God created the heavens and the earth.[474]

---

[473] I promise you; I am barefoot at the moment.

[474] Genesis 1:1. As an aside, there was a rather clever 11th century CE Jewish sage, Rabbi Shlomo Yitzchak ('Rashi'), who determined the duration of the current age

Not being as clever as Rashi (see footnote #2), all we can draw from this text is that God created everything that exists by divine fiat.[475] He is therefore transcendent – that is to say – independent from, and above, anything else that exists. Therefore, his power cannot be challenged, and his will cannot be thwarted.

So far so good. But exactly how did God create the universe? What power, process or mechanism did he use? According to the next verse, the Spirit of God was an active agent in the creation process:

> *The earth was without form, and void; and darkness was on the face of the deep. And the Spirit of God was hovering over the face of the waters.*[476]

Who or what is the 'Spirit of God'? As we saw in our 'Glassblower Man' illustration last chapter, God breathed his *n'shamah*, his life-force into Adam to create mankind. Just as it is the glassblower's breath that givers shape to the vessel he is creating; so it is God's divine breath, his *ruach*, supplied the power through which God shaped man to form his own image. Suppose God did the same thing with the universe to create it to his own divine satisfaction? With that thought percolating away in our minds, let's run with the theory that the Spirit of God is the manifestation of the power of God, shall we?

---

and the time of Messiah's coming based simply on the seven-word Hebrew text of this verse.

[475] Unlike the current Pope, whose popemobile is a Jeep. Mind you, the 1980s version used by Pope John Paul II was indeed made by Fiat.

[476] Genesis 1:2.

In the Book of Micah (one of the Twelve), the prophet condemns the false prophets of Judah and justifies his own ministry by contrast as follows:

> *But truly I am full of **power by the Spirit of the LORD**,*
> *and of justice and might, to declare to Jacob his*
> *transgression and to Israel his sin.*[477]

Micah appeals to the empowerment of his own prophetic ministry by means of the Spirit of God.

This is not an isolated incident. We find other occasions in the Tanakh where individuals receive empowerment for divine work by means of the Spirit of the LORD. For example, Bezalel, one of the artisans involved in the construction of the Tabernacle and its furnishings, was endowed with supernatural power for this undertaking:

> *Then the LORD spoke to Moses, saying: "See, I have called by name Bezalel the son of Uri, the son of Hur, of the tribe of Judah. And **I have filled him with the Spirit of God**, in wisdom, in understanding, in knowledge, and in all manner of workmanship, to design artistic works, to work in gold, in silver, in bronze, in cutting jewels for setting, in carving wood, and to work in all manner of workmanship."*[478]

One of the prophecies of Messiah we noted in Part Two foretells that he will be similarly empowered:

---

[477] Micah 3:8, emphasis mine.

[478] Exodus 31:1–5 – emphasis mine. See also Exodus 35:30–33.

The Spirit of the LORD shall rest upon Him, the Spirit of wisdom and understanding, the Spirit of counsel and might, the Spirit of knowledge and of the fear of the LORD.[479]

The Spirit of God is the Power of God

Soooooo, we have a *prima facie* case for God's Spirit, his *ruach,* being the **power** of God in this created world of ours. And that strengthens the supposition that the Spirit was a necessary instrument in the creation. We have seen that the *ruach* was *present* in creation 'hovering' over the face of the waters (Genesis 1:2). Was that a passive role?

The word translated 'hover' is the Hebrew term רָחַף (*rachaph*). Other translations may use different English words.[480] Some believe that the action involved can be better described by that of a bird 'brooding' over its nest.[481] However, the verb uses the *piel* stem, which means an active and intensive action.[482] If the analogy of a bird is to be used, this is not the effortless soaring of an eagle; this hovering eagle is moving its wings to remain aloft.

Where does God Live?

---

[479] Isaiah 11:2. I agree with my Christian brethren that Yeshua was Messiah (ben Yoseph). But if he is also the second person of the Triune God, why would he need God's supernatural empowerment in order to fear the LORD? Note also Isaiah 61:1 cp. Luke 4:18.

[480] E.g., KJV 'moved'. This isn't entirely pukka. The verb is a participle and should include the '-ing' suffix, if possible. Thus, NASB, RSV: 'moving'.

[481] Perhaps on the basis of Deuteronomy 32:11.

[482] For example, 'kill' is an active term [was killed would be the passive version], the intensive is a stronger form of kill e.g. 'slaughter'.

No, that's not meant to be a trick question, nor is there any need for guesswork, the scriptures provide the answer for us. At the dedication of the Temple, King Solomon's prayer included the following:

And may You hear the supplication of Your servant and of Your people Israel, when they pray toward this place. Hear in **heaven**[483] **Your dwelling place***; and when You hear, forgive.*[484]

But, earlier in the same prayer, Solomon acknowledged that the one true God was somewhat bigger than your average pagan deity:

But will God indeed dwell on the earth? Behold, heaven and the heaven of heavens cannot contain You. How much less this temple which I have built![485]

And, as God himself states:

Thus says the LORD: *"Heaven is My throne, and earth is My footstool. Where is the house that you will build Me? And where is the place of My rest?*[486]

God is speaking poetically in the above text, but even if it were a literal description of his dwelling-place, how is that theologians can claim that God is omnipresent?

---

[483] Hebrew: הַשָּׁמַיִם (*ha'shamayim*) - literally 'the heavens'.

[484] 1 Kings 8:30, emphasis mine. Also in verses 39, 43, 49.

[485] 1 Kings 8:27.

[486] Isaiah 66:1.

Again, the answer is simply that the bible says so:

The eyes of the LORD are in every place, keeping watch on the evil and the good.[487]

"Am I a God near at hand," says the LORD, "And not a God afar off? Can anyone hide himself in secret places, so I shall not see him?" says the LORD; "Do I not fill heaven and earth?" says the LORD.[488]

The Spirit of God is the Presence of God

So, how can God dwell in heaven and still be present everywhere else? King David knew the answer:

*Where can I go from **Your Spirit**? Or where can I flee from **Your presence**? If I ascend into heaven, You are there; If I make my bed in hell, behold, You are there. If I take the wings of the morning, and dwell in the uttermost parts of the sea, even there Your hand shall lead me, and Your right hand shall hold me.*[489]

Elsewhere David equates the presence of God in his life with the 'Holy Spirit':

Do not cast me away from Your presence, and do not take Your Holy Spirit from me.[490]

---

[487] Proverbs 15:3.

[488] Jeremiah 23:23-24.

[489] Psalm 139:7-10 – emphasis mine.

[490] Psalm 51:1.

The term 'your Holy Spirit' could also be translated 'your spirit/wind/breath of holiness'. [491] Either way, it is not unreasonable to see from the above text that the terms 'Holy Spirit' and 'Spirit of God' are synonyms, with the latter term being more common in the Tanakh.

Based on these texts, we must acknowledge that the Spirit of God is his [omni]presence. That is, God dwells in heaven; and his Spirit, his *ruach,* his divine breath, is his presence which extends throughout all creation.

God is Not a Man[492]

Having used the glassblower illustration of the creation of man in chapter one and developed that a little further in the model of creation, it is evident that we can't push this too far in understanding the makeup of God.

To begin with, the spirit/*ruach* of man provides him with knowledge of self and of his creator, but it is utterly incapable of omnipresence or knowledge beyond that which he has encountered. Moreover, a man's spirit has no power beyond himself. In contrast, God's *ruach,* as well as being his power and presence, remains sentient – better still – omniscient throughout all of creation. Isaiah asks the rhetorical question:

Who has directed the Spirit of the Lord, or as His counsellor has taught Him? With whom did He take counsel, and who instructed Him, and taught Him in the path of justice?

---

[491] Hebrew: רוּחַ קָדְשְׁךָ (*ruach qadeshkha*).

[492] Numbers 23:19a.

Who taught Him knowledge, and showed Him the way of understanding? [493]

This would be a meaningless text, if the Spirit of God was an impersonal force, rather than an extension, or part, of God himself.

This is not the same thing as saying the Holy Spirit is a person, and a third of the divine Godhead.

So, What's the Bottom Line?

God is not the same as us, but neither is he divided into three selves. His *ruach* is his omniscient, omnipresent, omnipotent self which extends throughout the creation. Or, to put it more simply, the Spirit of God of is his power and presence.

---

[493] Isaiah 40:13–14.

Chapter Three:
The Word of God

I have suggested that the Spirit of God is his sentient power and presence throughout creation, and that the same Spirit was the power behind creation, we now come to the Word of God. On what basis did the Spirit of God go ahead and create the universe? And how do we know that the final product was precisely what God had in mind?

Again, we must turn to the creation narrative. The third and fourth verses of the first chapter of Genesis provides the answers to both of those questions:

Then **God said,** *"Let there be light"; and there was light. And God saw the light, that* **it was good**...[494]

The Psalmist echoes this reality:

By the word of the LORD *the heavens were made, and all the host of them by the breath of His mouth.*[495]

God commanded that the universe be created, and it was accomplished to his total satisfaction by the power of his Spirit.

---

[494] Genesis 1:3–4a – emphasis mine.

[495] Psalm 33:6– emphasis mine.

The Mishnah expands on this reality by declaring that it was through ten 'utterances' that God created the world:

> *By ten utterances was the world created. What does this teach; for could not it have been created by one utterance?—The punishment of the wicked who destroy the world that was created by ten utterances, and the good reward of the righteous who sustain the world that was created by ten utterances.*[496]

Not only that, but among the various daily blessings [497] available to religious Jews, there is a general blessing said over food (not including grain) or drink (not including wine). It's called the *Sh'hakol,*[498] and can be translated into English as follows:

> *Blessed are you, Lord our God, King of the Universe, who by his word brings about all things.*

There's no doubt that all that is, exists purely because God has spoken.

God's Word is His Will

We might say that God's word is his **will** expressed. God **said**, "Let there be light", and that's precisely what took place. You and I are similar in this regard. We routinely express our

---

[496] m.*Avot.*5:1.

[497] Hebrew: בְּרָכוֹת (b'rachot). These are daily prayers of gratitude offered to God on various occasions e.g. dining, waking, tying t'fillin (phylacteries), before and after Torah study.

[498] Loosely translated: 'that's everything'.

will, desires or preferences through the facility of speech e.g. placing an order from the menu at a restaurant. The difference between ourselves and the Almighty God is that, while our breath provides the motive force for our words, it has neither sentience nor intrinsic power.

To illustrate, if I were to say, "Let there be a giraffe in my lounge room," that may express my desire, but would not have the power to place *giraffa camelopardalis*[499] beside my coffee table.

[At least I don't think so. Hang on a tick, let me try it... Nope, didn't work.]

But, if God were to do the same thing, a giraffe would find itself in my lounge room to our mutual astonishment.[500]

God's Written Word is His Will

Now, when we hear the expression 'the word of God' we tend to think of the holy scriptures, and with good reason. Just as I can express my will in written form, so the bible is God's written will for mankind. From the ninth chapter of Genesis, as we have noted earlier, God expressed his will for all humanity in the Noachide Covenant — those principles that Judaism formalised into seven laws. At Mount Sinai, God entered into a formal covenant with the descendants of Jacob.

---

[499] An attempt at showing off my grasp of Latin animal names. Well, to tell you the truth, I looked it up to try and sound like an intellectual.

[500] And a degree of concern on my part. I scarcely have enough grass to feed my sheep at this time of year and I'm certain that a giraffe would consume about thirty times daily what a single ovine does. Mind you, the giraffe is actually a kosher beast (split-hooved ruminant), and that's a lot of meat for the freezer. Now, there's a thought...

His will for them was expressed in the Torah and remains his will for the Jewish people to this day.

But wait, there's more…

God's Speaks His Will to Individuals

God has communicated his will – by his spoken word to individuals, as the biblical text records. He spoke to Adam, both before and after the man's sin:

> And the LORD God commanded the man, saying, "Of every tree of the garden you may freely eat; but of the tree of the knowledge of good and evil you shall not eat, for in the day that you eat of it you shall surely die." [501]

> Then to Adam [God] said, "Because you have heeded the voice of your wife, and have eaten from the tree of which I commanded you, saying, 'You shall not eat of it': "Cursed is the ground for your sake; in toil you shall eat of it all the days of your life." [502]

God spoke to Noah:

> Then God spoke to Noah, saying, "Go out of the ark, you and your wife, and your sons and your sons' wives with you." [503]

---

[501] Genesis 2:16–17.

[502] Genesis 3:17

[503] Genesis 8:15–16.

He spoke to Abram:

> Now the LORD had said to Abram: "Get out of your
> country, from your family and from your father's house, to
> a land that I will show you."[504]

And he spoke to Moses before and after the giving of the
Torah:

> And God spoke to Moses and said to him: "I am the
> LORD."[505]

> Then the LORD said to Moses, "Depart and go up from
> here, you and the people whom you have brought out of
> the land of Egypt, to the land of which I swore to Abraham,
> Isaac, and Jacob, saying, 'To your descendants I will give
> it.'"[506]

God Speaks His Will through Individuals

Throughout biblical history, God has appointed individuals
as prophets – his spokesmen through whom he communicates
his will to groups of people. There were prophets who
conveyed God's will to the king, during the monarchy:

> But it happened that night that the word of the LORD came
> to Nathan, saying, "Go and tell My servant David, 'Thus

---

[504] Genesis 12:1.

[505] Exodus 6:12.

[506] Exodus 33:1.

says the LORD: "Would you build a house for Me to dwell in?"' [507]

to the people of the northern kingdom of Israel following the division, even through an individual who had not previously been assigned a prophetic role:

"...I was no prophet, nor was I a son of a prophet, but I was a sheepbreeder and a tender of sycamore fruit. Then the LORD took me as I followed the flock, and the LORD said to me, 'Go, prophesy to My people Israel.'" [508]

to the people of the southern kingdom of Judah prior to the exile:

Therefore thus says the Lord GOD of hosts: "O My people, who dwell in Zion, do not be afraid of the Assyrian. He shall strike you with a rod and lift up his staff against you, in the manner of Egypt." [509]

and to the people of Judah in captivity:

Then He said to me, "The iniquity of the house of Israel and Judah is exceedingly great, and the land is full of bloodshed, and the city full of perversity; for they say, 'The LORD has forsaken the land, and the LORD does not see!'" [510]

and afterwards:

---

[507] 2 Samuel 7:4-5.

[508] Amos 7:14b-15.

[509] Isaiah 10:24.

[510] Ezekiel 9:9.

Then the word of the LORD came by Haggai the prophet, saying, "Is it time for you yourselves to dwell in your paneled houses, and this temple to lie in ruins?" Now therefore, thus says the LORD of hosts: "Consider your ways!" [511]

God Speaks to Those Who do not Know Him

In the Tanakh we read of the prophet Jonah who was dispatched (with some reluctance)[512] to Nineveh, the capital of the pagan nation of Assyria, to call them to repentance:

Now the word of the LORD came to Jonah the son of Amittai, saying, "Arise, go to Nineveh, that great city, and cry out against it; for their wickedness has come up before Me." [513]

The prophet Nahum had no word of criticism for Israel but prophesied strongly against the wickedness of the Assyrian people. For example:

"Behold, I am against you [Nineveh]," says the LORD of hosts, "I will burn your chariots in smoke, and the sword shall devour your young lions; I will cut off your prey from the earth, and the voice of your messengers shall be heard no more." [514]

---

[511] Haggai 1:3–5.

[512] His experience casts the idea of eating 'seafood' in a totally new light.

[513] Jonah 1:1–2.

[514] Nahum 2:13.

So, What's the Bottom Line?

In this chapter we postulated that God's **word** is his **will** as revealed in the scriptures, as spoken to individuals, and as through the prophets to his people and others.

Thus, we have one God and only one God whose Spirit is his power and presence to fulfil his word which is his will throughout creation. How, then, could the Christian church come up with the idea of a trinity? Well, ancient Jewish thinking is partly responsible for the development of the gentile Christian theological position.

Let me explain...

Chapter Four:
God: Transcendent or Immanent?

The ancient Jews struggled with the concept of transcendent God interacting in some direct encounter with mortal man, just as we did in the first chapter or two of the previous section. On the one hand, scripture declares that no man can see God's face and live (Exodus 33:20). But, on the other, there are occasions in Holy Writ where that very thing appears to have happened – and without lethal consequences to the individual concerned. For instance, we read that after his fairly unusual nocturnal bout of wrestling:

> *So Jacob called the name of the place Peniel: "For I have seen God face to face, and my life is preserved."* [515]

How can these apparently contradictory statements be part of the divinely inspired Torah?

Concreting the Abstract

We noted in Part One that Greeksmen are content to ponder abstract principles, while Hebrewsmen prefer to reduce the abstract to a concrete form. The term that describes attributing concrete features to an abstract concept is (believe

---

[515] Genesis 32:30 – Hebrew: פְּנִיאֵל *(p'niel)*, as previously noted, means 'face of God'.

it or not) to 'hypostasise'.[516] In the Book of Proverbs, Israel's wise king hypostasises the abstract principle of wisdom,[517] awarding it feminine personhood:

> *Wisdom calls aloud outside; she raises her voice in the open squares.*[518]

> *Wisdom has built her house, she has hewn out her seven pillars; she has slaughtered her meat, she has mixed her wine, she has also furnished her table.*[519]

This practice of personifying wisdom is also apparent in some apocryphal texts. Addressing God, the author of *The Wisdom of Solomon*[520] states:

> *With you is wisdom, she who knows your works and was present when you made the world; she understands what is pleasing in your sight and what is right according to your commandments.*[521]

---

[516] That's a piece of trivia you can keep – and it comes to you free of charge. But wait, there's more! With every sixth piece of trivia, you get a free set of steak knives. Act now!

[517] Once more there is a difference in the cultural understanding of wisdom. In Greek thought it is the ability to solve problems based on knowledge and experience. In Hebraic thought, wisdom חָכְמָה (*chokmah*) is possessing the skills for righteous living... sorry, I just thought you'd like to know that... I'm not sure why, really.

[518] Proverbs 1:20.

[519] Proverbs 9:1-2.

[520] Probably written first century BCE.

[521] Wisdom 9:9.

What may be the most expansive treatise on 'wisdom personified' is found in chapters seven and eight of the same book. Just the first of thirty verses is reproduced below:

> *There is in her a spirit that is intelligent, holy, unique, manifold, subtle, mobile, clear, unpolluted, distinct, invulnerable, loving the good, keen, irresistible, beneficent, humane, steadfast, sure, free from anxiety, all-powerful, overseeing all, and penetrating through all spirits that are intelligent, pure, and altogether subtle.*[522]

Why am I telling you this?

Read on…

The Personification of the Word of God

As a partial solution to the transcendence–immanence dilemma, the practice of substituting the 'word of the Lord' for God himself appeared in some apocryphal writings. Here is a classic example, also from *The Wisdom of Solomon:*

> *For while gentle silence enveloped all things, and night in its swift course was now half gone, **your all-powerful word leaped from heaven**, from the royal throne, into the midst of the land that was doomed, a stern warrior carrying the sharp sword of your authentic command, and stood and filled all things with death, and touched heaven while standing on the earth.*[523]

---

[522] Wisdom 7:22.

[523] Wisdom 18:14–16, emphasis mine.

A not uncommon biblical phenomenon is when the word of God comes to a prophet. We noted one example in the previous chapter when:

...the word of the LORD came to Nathan...[524]

and similar examples abound.[525] I had always presumed that this expression meant that God spoke, and the prophet heard his voice. However, in the Second Book of Baruch, a first-century CE Jewish writing, the implication is that word of God (personified) was despatched to the prophet as God's intermediary:

*And it came to pass in the twenty-fifth year of Jeconiah, king of Judah, that the word of the Lord came to Baruch, the son of Neriah, **and said to him**: "Have you seen all that this people are doing to me, that the evils which these two tribes which remained have done are greater than (those of) the ten tribes which were carried away captive?"*[526]

We can go back a couple of centuries to the Book of Enoch wherein we find a similar statement:

*And in those days the word of God came to me and **said to me**, "Noah, your lot has come up to me, a lot without blame, a lot of love and uprightness."*[527]

---

[524] 2 Samuel 7:4b.

[525] Over 100 instances in the Tanakh.

[526] 2 Baruch 2:1-2, emphasis mine.

[527] Enoch 67:1 – emphasis mine.

But the personification of God's word originated earlier than the apocrypha. If the Targums accurately reflect Jewish understanding during the exile, God's word personified has its origins during the Babylonian/Persian era, as we shall see next chapter...

Chapter Five:
Thanks for the Memras[528]

In Part Two we discussed the Targums – those Aramaic translations of the Tanakh which included the gloss of those who composed, recited or scribed them. There were two Targums originating in Babylon: Onqelos was the translation of the Torah and Jonathan comprised the prophets. The western Targums included Neofiti dedicated to the Torah and Pseudo-Jonathan which covered most of the Tanakh.

Within these documents we find many instances of the word *Memra*, which simply means 'word' (or 'speech') in Aramaic.[529] Uncomfortable with God interacting directly with man, post-exilic Judaism began to substitute the word Memra as a metonym for God when he acted within our meagre dimensions. This word substitute was not intended as an anthropomorphism – the Memra does not assume human form. However, on many occasions in the Tanakh the surrogate use of Memra is in circumstances suggestive of this unintentional perspective.

In this and the next chapter, I want to examine all the texts in the Targums to get a proper handle on what functions the Memra fulfils.

---

[528] With due apologies to Bob Hope & Shirley Ross's 1938 hit song of a similar title. I suspect they plagiarised it from this book.

[529] Aramaic: מֵימְרָא

Did I say **all the texts?**

Alas, that's exactly what I said. However, the good news is that I won't have **you** explore all the [literally] hundreds and hundreds of occurrences. What I'll do, as we proceed from the first example of Memra in the Aramaic paraphrase of the Torah, is to limit subsequent instances to those that add to our understanding. Hopefully, that means that, as we go further, there will be fewer texts that we need to review.

Having said that, it may be a mostly pedestrian process for those of you who prefer brevity to exhaustiveness. If that describes you, I suggest you read a page or two and then skip to the 'bottom line' summaries at the end of this and the following chapter.

Enjoy – If you can…

Memra in the Torah

Memra appears more than two hundred times in the Torah of Targum Onqelos and there are over four hundred instances in Neofiti. In the rest of this chapter we will consider the Memra in the Torah. We'll examine Onqelos first, as it is probably the oldest extant version and list the activities and responsibilities of the Memra.

Targum Onqelos

The first appearance of Memra in Targum Onqelos occurs when fallen Adam and Eve heard God walking in the garden:

Then they heard the voice of the Memra of the Lord God walking in the garden towards the decline of the day; so Adam and his wife hid themselves from before the Lord God within a tree of the garden.[530]

From this text the Memra assumes the personal abilities of walking and speech.

A little later in Genesis, God attributes creation to his Memra:

then the Lord regretted through his Memra that He had made man on earth...[531]

In Genesis chapter nine, the Memra is established as the mediator[532] of the Noachide covenant with all living creatures.

So the Lord said to Noah, "This is the sign of the covenant which I have established between My Memra and all flesh that is upon the earth."[533]

The Memra becomes the source of strength for Abram:

---

[530] Genesis 3:8 TgOnq.

[531] Genesis 6:6a TgOnq.

[532] That word has just given me a brilliant idea for an automotive innovation! The *mediator,* which not only keeps the coolant at an appropriate temperature, but can also act as a media-player. The world's richest men have obtained their wealth through seizing possibilities like this.

[533] Genesis 9:15 TgOnq. In fact, the Memra is also party to the Abrahamic Covenant (Genesis 17:7-11 TgOnq).

After these matters, the word of the Lord was with Abram in a prophecy, as follows: "Do not fear, Abram, My Memra shall he your strength, your reward shall be very great." [534]

and supplies aid to those who enjoy the LORD's favour:

And the Memra of the Lord was at the aid of [Ishmael], and he grew up and lived in the wilderness, and he became an archer boy. [535]

The Memra can be sworn by as a token of sincerity – not just by an dividual but, curiously enough, by God as well. Compare Abimelech's words to Abraham:

Now therefore swear to me here by the Memra of the Lord, that you will not deal falsely with me... [536]

with God's words to Abraham:

And he said, "By My Memra, I swear, says the Lord, because you have done this thing and have not withheld your son, your only one. [537]

One can even pray in the name of the Memra:

...and there Abram prayed[l] in the name of the Memra of the Lord.

---

[534] Genesis 15:1 TgOnq cp. Genesis 12:7 TgNeo.

[535] Genesis 21:20 TgOnq.

[536] Genesis 21:23 TgOnq. the Memra can also be invoked as a witness between parties e.g., Genesis 31:49-50.

[537] Genesis 22:16 TgOnq.

In the Book of Exodus, it is implied that the Memra would dwell between the cherubim in the Tabernacle:

And I will appoint My Memra {to be} there for you, and I will discuss with you from above the cover from between the two cherubs which are on top of the Ark of Testimony, all that I shall command you for the Israelites.[538]

The Memra continues to be a party to the covenant and its sign – this time the Sinai Covenant:

Now you should speak with the Israelites saying, "Nevertheless, you should observe My Sabbath days, for it is a sign between My Memra and you for your generations to realize that I am the Lord who has consecrated you."[539]

Because Memra is the solution to the God-entering-man's-domain problem, it is with the Memra that God shields Moses from as the LORD's glory passes by (in the Hebrew text it is the LORD's hand):

So when My Glory passes by, I will place you in a cleft of the rock and will shield you with My Memra until I have passed by.[540]

The Books of Leviticus through Deuteronomy in Onqelos confirm what we have already discovered but add little to any further understanding of the Memra.

---

[538] Exodus 25:22 TgOnq 29:42-43 confirms this implication.

[539] Exodus 31:13 TgOnq cp 31:17.

[540] Genesis 33:22 TgOnq.

Targum Neofiti

As noted above, Targum Neofiti has around twice as many references to the Memra as Onqelos. We'll now look at those texts which provide *additional* information on the Memra, not noted in Onqelos.

To begin, Neofiti includes the Memra [along with wisdom] as the agent of creation in the very first verse of scripture:

From the beginning with wisdom the Memra of the Lord created and perfected the heavens and the earth.[541]

In Genesis chapter seventeen, the Memra is identified as the redeemer of the descendants of Abraham, through his chosen line:

And I will give to you and to your sons after you the land of your sojournings, all the land of Canaan, as an everlasting inheritance. And I will be for them in my Memra a redeemer God.[542]

The Memra is also the agent of God's wrath, delivering judgment when God's justice demands it:

And the Memra of the Lord made sulphur and fire come down upon Sodom and Gomorrah from before the Lord, from the heavens.[543]

---

[541] Genesis 1:1 TgNeo. In the rest of the creation narrative, the Memra is the sole agent. Perhaps the intent of Genesis 1:1 is to convey that God used his facility of wisdom in creating the universe by his Memra?

[542] Genesis 17:8 TgNeo.

[543] Genesis 19:24 TgNeo.

And in chapter twenty-four Abraham both prays and *worships* in the name of the Memra:

> *And Abraham worshiped and prayed in the name of the Memra of the Lord...*[544]

In chapter twenty-eight, any uncertainty that God truly does indwell his Memra is removed:

> *And behold,* **I in my Memra** *am with you and shall keep you wherever you go; and I will make you return to this land, because my Memra shall not forsake you until I have done what I spoke to you.*[545]

By the time we get to Exodus,[546] we find the Memra as a substitute for the Hebrew text's 'Angel of the LORD':

> *... and the Memra of the Lord called to him from the midst of the [burning] thorn bush and said to him: "Moses, Moses."*[547]

and, just like Onqelos, Neofiti has nothing more to add to our list from the rest of the Torah.

---

[544] Genesis 24:14a TgNeo.

[545] Genesis 28:15 TgNeo – emphasis mine.

[546] Here's a little-known piece of music trivia for you: *By the Time We Get to Exodus* was the original title of Jimmy Webb's 1965 composition, made famous by country singer Glen Campbell in 1967 under the revised name *By the Time I Get to Phoenix.*

[547] Exodus 3:4b TgNeo.

Targum Pseudo-Jonathan

There is a text in Genesis four which, although it doesn't add much to our understanding of the Memra, it does assist in understanding a puzzling text. The Hebrew text reads:

And as for Seth, to him also a son was born; and he named him Enosh. Then men began to call on the name of the LORD.[548]

The 'name of the LORD' appears prior to, and after the creation of Adam and Seth's line produced godly offspring through to Noah and his sons.[549] Nonetheless, chapter six of Genesis, as we know, describes the wickedness of mankind[550] culminating in the destruction of [almost] all flesh by the flood. So, how is it that things went so pear-shaped after men began to call on the name of the LORD? It could be that Pseudo-Jonathan has the explanation:

*And to Seth also a son was born, and he called his name Enosh. That was the generation in which they began to go astray, making idols for themselves and **calling their idols** by the name of the Memra of the Lord.*[551]

---

[548] Genesis 4:26.

[549] Genesis 5:6–32.

[550] Not to mention those naughty old angelic beings, the 'Watchers' and their fondness for the ladies. And yes, I do hold to that viewpoint on the origin of the *n'philim.*

[551] Genesis 4:26 TgPsjon (emphasis mine). By the way, we know that Esau was a hunter and turned up at his father's deathbed after the blessing of the firstborn had been obtained, through skulduggery, by his brother Isaac. He'd even gone to the trouble of bringing a jolly nice casserole to his dad. Pseudo-Jonathan informs us that the Memra preventing Esau from finding clean game and that the casserole was

Moving on, in chapter one of this section we saw that God breathes his 'breath of life' into all living creatures. Pseudo-Jonathan attributes this empowerment to the Memra:

Let the Memra of the Lord, which rules over the soul of man and from whom has been given the breath of life to all flesh...[552]

In Deuteronomy chapter four, we find the Ten Words (aka Ten Commandments) referred to as the 'Ten Memras',[553] returning us to the idea earlier in this part that the word of God is the will of God. To that we can add confirmation that the Memra is the word and will of God.

The thirty-second chapter of Deuteronomy contains a promise that the LORD will atone for his people by means of his Memra:

...he, by his Memra, will make atonement for the sins of his land and of his people.[554]

And that's all folks, from the Torah regarding God's Memra in the Aramaic Targums.

---

actually dog stew. Eeeuuuwww. Nothing to do with our topic of course, but you know...?

[552] Numbers 27:16a TgPsjon.

[553] Deuteronomy 4:13 TgPsjon.

[554] Deuteronomy 32:43b TgPsjon.

So, What's the Bottom Line?

In the exilic and post-exilic period Judaism adopted the idea of a mediator, or agent, or manifestation of God in his dealings within our time-space dimension. This intermediary was the Memra, the personification of the word of God.

Although there are hundreds of references to the Memra in the Torah, as written in the Targums (with its non-inspired gloss), there are only half a dozen or so which bear relevance to our discussion. Nevertheless, Still, we've got the rest of the Tanakh to investigate. Perhaps we can learn some more about the Memra?

Let's see...

Chapter Six:
Memra in the Rest of the Tanakh

In Chapter Five we discovered six significant things that describe the function of God's post-exilic mediator, the Memra. In this chapter we will continue our investigation of the Targums, recording only new information as we come to it. We will begin with the Prophets and conclude with the Writings.

Ready?

Former Prophets

In the Book of Joshua, it is the Memra who will fight on Israel's behalf:

> And there was nothing like that day before it and after it, that the prayer of a man was accepted before the Lord, for the Lord by his Memra waged battle for Israel.[555]

And in their conquest of Canaan, it was the Memra who apportioned the territory to the sons of Israel:

> To Caleb the son of Jephunneh he gave a portion in the midst of the sons of Judah according to the Memra of the

---

[555] Joshua 10:14 TgJon.

Lord to Joshua—the city of Arba the father of the giants, that is, Hebron.[556]

According to the Second Samuel, it was the Memra that anointed David as king:

...David the son of Jesse spoke; and the utterance of the man who was raised to kingship, the anointed by the Memra of the God of Jacob...[557]

Latter Prophets

In Isaiah the Memra is linked with God's salvation:

Behold, in the Memra of the God of my salvation I trust, and will not be shaken; for the awesome one, the LORD, is my strength and my song; he has spoken by his Memra, and he has become for me a saviour.[558]

and is the hope of Israel:

In that time a man will rely on the service of his maker, and his eyes will hope in the Memra of the Holy One of Israel.[559]

---

[556] Joshua 15:13 TgJon

[557] 2 Samuel 23:1b TgJon.

[558] Isaiah 12:2 TgIsa.

[559] Isaiah 17:7 TgIsa.

As we go further in Isaiah, the Memra is the gatherer[560] of Israel:

Seek and search in the book of the LORD: not one of these is missing; no female is without her mate. For by his Memra they will be gathered, and by his pleasure they will draw near.[561]

and the means by which Israel will be justified and glorified:

In the Memra of the LORD all the seed of Israel shall be justified and glorified.[562]

Lastly, the Memra is the comforter of Israel in Isaiah sixty-six:

As one whom his mother comforts, so my Memra will comfort you; you shall be comforted in Jerusalem.[563]

In Jeremiah the Memra will administer the exile:
As I live, says the Lord, even if Coniah the son of Jehoiakim, the king of the tribe of the house of Judah, were like the engraving of the signet-ring on my right hand, even from there I would exile you by my Memra.[564]

and the return from exile:

---

[560] In the Hebrew text, it is the Spirit who performs this function.

[561] Isaiah 34:16 TgIsa.

[562] Isaiah 45:25 TgIsa.

[563] Isaiah 66:13 TgIsa.

[564] Jeremiah 22;4 TgJer.

And it will be that, after I shall have exiled them, I will return in my Memra and have pity on them and make them return, each man to his inheritance and each to his land.[565]

as well as being the agent of blessing in the renewed covenant.

And I will make an everlasting covenant for them, for my Memra shall not return from them to do good for them...[566]

The Book of Ezekiel contains what may be a messianic prophecy, in which the Memra will establish the Messiah:

Thus says the Lord God, "I Myself will bring near a child from the kingdom of the house of David which is likened to the lofty cedar, and I will establish him from among his children's children; I will anoint and establish him by My Memra on a high and exalted mountain.[567]

The Twelve

There's just one text in The Twelve (Minor Prophets) that is relevant to our discussion. Hosea confirms David's deathbed statement that it is the Memra who appoints Israel's kings:

They have made kings but not through my Memra. They have made princes but not according to my will...[568]

---

[565] Jeremiah 12:5 TgJer cp. 24:6.

[566] Jeremiah 32:40a TgJer.

[567] Ezekiel 17:22 TgEze.

[568] Hosea 8:4a Tg.MP.

The Writings

There are no extant Targums for Daniel and Ezra-Nehemiah. The Targums of Proverbs, Song of Songs, Lamentations and Esther [569] contain no references to the Memra. The Memra is mentioned in Job, Ruth, and Ecclesiastes but the occurrences add nothing to our understanding thus far. That just leaves the Psalms and Chronicles.

In the Psalms, the Memra is to be trusted for a share in the Land:

Look to the Memra of the LORD, and keep his way; and he will exalt you to possess the land... [570]

In Second Chronicles, it is the spirit of the Memra which sustains creation:

...The heavens are the throne of his glory and the earth a footstool before him, and the deep and the whole world are sustained by the spirit of his Memra... [571]

---

[569] There are two Targums of Ether known as *Rishon* and *Sheni* (Hebrew: 'first' and 'second').

[570] Psalm 34:17a TgPsa.

[571] 2 Chronicles 2:5b TgChr.

So, What's the Bottom Line?

Having extended our study of the Memra in the rest of the Tanakh (as found in the Aramaic Targums) we discovered only a handful of additional characteristics which we may add to those we found in the Torah. A consolidated list of the activities and responsibilities of the Memra from all the Targums available is written below:

1. The Memra created the universe.

2. The Memra dwelt between the cherubim in the Tabernacle.

3. The Memra mediates God's covenants with mankind.

4. The Memra is the source of aid to, and blessing upon, God's people.

5. The Memra executes God's judgment on the wicked.

6. The Memra is Israel's redeemer and means of atonement.

7. The Memra fights on Israel's behalf.

8. The Memra is the one who justifies and glorifies Israel.

9. The Memra is comforter of Israel.

10. The Memra apportions the territory to the tribes of Israel within the Land.

11. The Memra drove the exiles from the Land and will return them to the Land.

12. The Memra is the agent of blessing in the renewed covenant.

13. The Memra appoints kings and may be the one who establishes the Messiah.

That's all very well (I hear you say), but what's this got to do with the Christian doctrine of the trinity?

Next chapter...

Chapter Seven:
To the Trinity and Beyond

Let me begin with a disclaimer. The purpose of this chapter is not to foist a remodelled trinity onto my Jewish readers. Nor is it to unnecessarily offend my Christian readers. Rather, I am seeking, once again, to diminish the differences that separate our camps. If both groups, at the end of this chapter can say, "Well, I don't agree with what he says, but I can see that it makes a little bit of sense," this chapter will have achieved its aim.

I've suggested to you that Spirit of God is his sentient power and presence throughout the universe. Then we examined the word of God as being his will for creation. He even explained his will for us in written form in the holy scriptures. After that, we spent considerable time looking at post-exilic Judaism's personification of God's word as the Memra, which appears hundreds of times in the gloss of the Aramaic Targums.

Let's move on...

Who was Yeshua?

If we consider the life of this man as revealed in the four gospels of the Apostolic Writings, we should be able to agree that he was a Torah-observant sage as a minimum point of agreement.

We've seen previously that, of the four gospels, John's narrative was the last written. Indeed, it may have been the last of all the Apostolic Writings, being penned in the late first-century CE. That's because John, a young man who accompanied Yeshua through his ministry, outlived all the other followers.[572] That being the case, his gospel would have content that was based on his many years of theological reflection on the things he saw and experienced.

John's account begins with the longstanding Jewish belief that word of God, the *Memra*, is a metonym for God in his dealings with mankind:

> *In the beginning was the Word, and the Word was with God, and the Word was God. He was in the beginning with God.*[573]

Writing in Greek, the Apostle John uses the term *logos,*[574] the Greek term for 'word', not the Aramaic term Memra.

Much has been written about the Jewish philosopher Philo of Alexandria's use of the term *logos* in his attempt to harmonise Torah with Neoplatonist thought, and its influence on the Christian dogma of the trinity. But John the disciple was a fisherman from Galilee. Yes, he was exiled to Patmos by the Roman authorities and eventually settled and died in Ephesus in Asia Minor. Even so, his gospel narrative is unlikely to have been heavily influenced by the philosophical ideas of his Jewish contemporary in Alexandria, modern day Egypt.

---

[572] According to tradition, John was born in 6 CE in Bethsaida, Galilee and died around 100 CE in Ephesus, Asia Minor.

[573] John 1:1–2.

[574] Greek: λόγος

I submit that John had the concept of Memra in mind when he used the term *logos* in the prologue to his gospel. If we substitute Memra within the text, it is consistent with post-exilic Jewish thought:

In the beginning was the [Memra], and the [Memra] was with God, and the [Memra] was God. He was in the beginning with God.[575]

So far, so good, but the crux of John's gospel is revealed in the fourteenth verse of that first chapter:

And the [Memra] became flesh and dwelt among us...

In Jewish thought, the Memra was the personification of the word of God – his presence in the dimension of humanity and mediator therein. The Memra, as mentioned previously, was **not an anthropomorphic term in Judaism,** just a means by which God could interact with us. John's theology goes way beyond what his Jewish peers could have expected.

There's the rub...

John is declaring that Yeshua was the Memra, not simply in the form or appearance of a man. Rather he is arguing that Yeshua, in every sense a human being, was somehow God's Memra. That would mean that, as God's **word** his life would reflect God's **will** for humanity.

How could Yeshua, as a man, live a life that was an example for all mankind? The answer can be found in the three synoptic

---

[575] John 1:1–2.

gospels written prior to John's account. They describe Yeshua's 'baptism' by John the Immerser:

When He had been baptised, Jesus came up immediately from the water; and behold, the heavens were opened to Him, and He saw the Spirit of God descending like a dove and alighting upon Him.[576]

There You Have It

Yeshua, in my opinion, is not the Second Person of a Triune God. He was the Memra in the flesh, empowered by the Spirit of God, to complete God's will for his life.

I recognise that this perspective may be an absurdity to some of my readers – whether they be Jew. or Christian.

That's okay. I'm not saying that you are obliged to agree with me.

I'm asking my Jewish readers to consider it as less of a divisive wedge than the traditional Christian trinitarian model of God. I honestly contend that it preserves the monotheism of the *sh'ma,* while allowing Yeshua to be a historically unique Jew and, [from a Jewish perspective] may even elevate the erstwhile ludicrous possibility that Yeshua could be a candidate for the title of Son of David when this age concludes with the arrival of Messiah.

I'm asking my Christian readers to put aside two millennia of enshrined and defended-to-the-death theological dogma

---

[576] Matthew 3:16 also Mark 1:10; Luke 3:21-22.

and reconsider the trinitarian proof texts in the Apostolic Writings in the light of Yeshua as *Memra* and see that it preserves the Apostolic Writings as inspired scripture. Just about every instance in the Apostolic Writings that imply or state the deity of Yeshua can be explained by substitution of the word Memra.

Yeshua Created the World?

There are texts within the Apostolic Writings which exalt Yeshua to the status of Creator. Christians use these verses as proof of his Triune status. The primary proof text comes from the Apostle Paul's letter to the assembly at Colossae:

> *He [Yeshua] is the image of the invisible God, the firstborn over all creation. For by Him all things were created that are in heaven and that are on earth, visible and invisible, whether thrones or dominions or principalities or powers. All things were created through Him and for Him.*[577]

At first blush, this text supports traditional Christian dogma. However, if John was correct and Yeshua was the Memra in the flesh – the substitution is not inconsistent with post-exilic understanding of the word of God.

Let's pull this verse apart as we do so:

> *[The Memra] is the image of the invisible God...*

This was the function of the Memra in Jewish thought – to present a tangible form or presence of God in his interaction

---

[577] Colossians 1:15–16.

with humankind.[578] We find a similar statement regarding the [female] personification of wisdom in the apocryphal text, *The Wisdom of Solomon*:

> *For she is a breath of the power of God, and a pure emanation of the glory of the Almighty; therefore nothing defiled gains entrance into her. For she is a reflection of eternal light, a spotless mirror of the working of God, and* **an image of his goodness.**[579]

Yeshua is the Firstborn, Sort Of...

Much has been made of the next part of the text:

> *...the firstborn over all creation.*

especially in regard to the Greek word in Paul's letter, translated above as 'firstborn'.[580] It is argued that this word implies more than just the child who happens to arrive before any of his or her siblings. Since it is believed that Yeshua is the second person of the triune God, how could he have been 'born' – for that would imply that he, himself, was created.

The Greek word appears over a hundred-and-twenty times in the Septuagint – on almost every occasion it translates the

---

[578] In another of Paul's letters, Philippians, he notes that Yeshua was ἐν μορφῇ θεοῦ - in a form of God (Philippians 2:5), even as the Memra was a 'form of God'.

[579] Wisdom 7:25-26 emphasis mine.

[580] πρωτότοκος (*prototokos*)

Hebrew word *b'khor*,[581] or a cognate thereof. The meaning of the word is — surprise, surprise - 'firstborn' Here is its first appearance in the Tanakh:

> *Abel also brought of the **firstborn** of his flock...*[582]

Christians could capitalise on this translation as the same term is used of King David in the psalms:

> *He shall cry to Me, 'You are my Father, My God, and the rock of my salvation.' Also I will make him My firstborn, the highest of the kings of the earth.*[583]

and a case could be put that Yeshua is the greater 'son of David'. However, the Christian is obliged to make the term *prototokos* mean something other than 'firstborn'.

Here is a typical statement regarding the application of *prototokos* to Yeshua:

> The Greek word implied two things, priority to all creation and sovereignty over all creation. In the first meaning we see the absolute pre-existence of the Logos. Since our Lord existed before all created things, He must be uncreated. Since He is uncreated, He is eternal. Since He is eternal, He is God. Since He is God, He cannot be one of the emanations from deity of which the Gnostic

---

[581] Hebrew: בְּכוֹר also spelled בְּכֹר. On two occasions it translates פֶּטֶר (*peter*) meaning firstborn; one time רִאשׁוֹן (*rishon*) which means 'first' and is used to describe Esau who was the twin born *first*.

[582] Genesis 4:4a emphasis mine. In the Hebrew text it is בְּכֹר; πρωτότοκος in the LXX.

[583] Psalm 89:26-27. The word 'firstborn' is, again, the Hebrew בְּכֹר translated by πρωτότοκος in the LXX.

speaks...In the second meaning we see that He is the natural ruler, the acknowledged head of God's household...He is Lord of creation.[584]

Without wishing to cast any aspersions on the writer of that quote's superior knowledge of *Koine Greek,* it does appear just a bit convoluted to me. If we consider Yeshua's birth narrative, the word *prototokos* has the more common meaning:

And [Mary] *brought forth her firstborn* [prototokos] *Son, and wrapped Him in swaddling cloths, and laid Him in a manger, because there was no room for them in the inn.*[585]

In any case, a couple of verses later, Paul uses Yeshua's 'firstborn' status, metaphorically, to speak of his resurrection from the grave:

And He is ... the firstborn from the dead...[586]

Even the Apostle John, who penned Revelation, uses *prototokos* in this context:

John, to the seven churches which are in Asia: Grace to you and peace from Him who is and who was and who is to come, and from the seven Spirits who are before His throne, and from Jesus Christ, the faithful witness, the

---

[584] Wuest, Kenneth, *Word Studies in the Greek New Testament,* (Grand Rapids:Eerdmans, 1981),183.

[585] Luke 2:7.

[586] Colossians 1:18.

firstborn from the dead, and the ruler over the kings of the earth.[587]

So, What's the Bottom Line?

The bottom line is that the Apostolic Writings state that Yeshua was the word of God in the flesh. This is not inconsistent with the Jewish understanding of the Memra. Moreover, they teach that he was the firstborn i.e. the first one physically and permanently raised from the dead.[588]

My point is that, whether these claims are true or false, the do not contradict the fundamentals of Judaism in any significant way. The same cannot be said of the Christian dogma of the trinity. There is one and only one God; his Spirit is his sentient power and presence throughout creation, and his Memra became flesh in Yeshua to demonstrate his will for Israel. That's why Yeshua had to keep Torah.

Of course, there's another reason that Yeshua was Torah-observant, and that's what we'll examine in the final chapter in this section...

---

[587] Revelation 1:4-5, emphasis mine.

[588] In another letter, the Apostle Paul refers to him as the 'firstfruits' from the dead – 1 Corinthians 15:20.

Chapter Eight:
Of Covenants and Corporate Solidarities

The concept of a 'corporate solidarity' is a bit foreign to our modern western culture. However, in biblical times it was an accepted part of Jewish cultural understanding. A corporate solidarity is a significant individual within the group, nation or tribe. Here's the kicker:

> ## WHAT IS TRUE OF THE CORPORATE SOLIDARITY IS, SOMEHOW, ALSO TRUE FOR THE ENTIRE GROUP.

As I mentioned, this idea is at odds with our way of thinking, with our Western notions of self-reliance.

So, let me provide you with...

A Biblical Example

In the Book of Genesis, Jacob wrestled with the Angel of the Lord throughout the night. He was permanently disabled had his name changed to Israel in the process.[589] If we look at the Prophet Hosea's take on this event, over a thousand years later, he writes:

---

[589] Genesis 32:20–32.

*Yes, [Jacob] struggled with the Angel and prevailed; He wept, and sought favor from Him. He found Him in Bethel, and **there He spoke to us** – that is, the LORD God of hosts. The LORD is His memorable name.*[590]

The prophet is declaring that, in speaking to Jacob, the LORD was speaking to the entire nation. That is, Jacob was a corporate solidarity for all Israel according to this scripture. Earlier in Hosea, God speaks of Israel as the child he called out of Egypt:

When Israel was a child, I loved him, and out of Egypt I called My son.[591]

The rest of the passage confirms that by the individual Israel, God was referring to the entire nation who left Egypt under the leadership of Moses centuries later.

Covenants Revisited

As noted earlier in this writing, God has entered into covenant relationship with individuals, such as Abraham and King David and with groups – all mankind (descended from Noah) and Israel specifically at Mount Sinai.

The two kinds of covenant common to the ancient near east were the Royal Grant and the Suzerainty agreements.

---

[590] Hosea 12:4–5, emphasis mine.

[591] Hosea 11:1.

Royal Grant Covenant

In this type of covenant, a powerful ruler would bestow a lesser kingdom on a favoured individual with no fine print, that is, with no strings attached. A biblical example of this covenant is the one God made with Abraham in Genesis chapter twelve:

Now the LORD had said to Abram: "Get out of your country, from your family and from your father's house, to a land that I will show you. I will make you a great nation; I will bless you and make your name great; and you shall be a blessing. I will bless those who bless you, and I will curse him who curses you; and in you all the families of the earth shall be blessed." [592]

In this covenant God sovereignly promises Abram that he will give him the land; make him a great nation; that all the families of the earth would be blessed through him, and that God's favour or curse on others would depend on their attitude to Abram and his descendants. This covenant promise continues through Abram's chosen line of Isaac, Jacob and the twelve tribes of Israel.

There are no preconditions to this covenant – God simply bestowed his blessing upon this man Abram in a Royal Grant. Nonetheless, God did give Abram a sign or seal of the covenant grant:

This is My covenant which you shall keep, between Me and you and your descendants after you: Every male child among you shall be circumcised; and you shall be

---

[592] Genesis 12:1-3.

circumcised in the flesh of your foreskins, and it shall be a sign of the covenant between Me and you.[593]

Failure to comply with this instruction would result in being 'cut off' from the covenant people.[594]

Suzerainty Covenant

In the other major type of covenant, a powerful ruler (the Suzerain) permits a lesser ruler – known as the 'Vassal' – to govern over a region as long as the latter keeps all the rules imposed by the former.[595] This kind of covenant was common in the case of military conquest. The victor would allow the conquered ruler to continue governing his realm provided that, as the vassal, he paid his taxes to the suzerain and imposed the latter's policies upon his subjects. Any uprising by the vassal would result in swift punishment.

The Sinai Covenant was of this nature. God promised Israel that he would bless them, so long as they followed the fine print contained within the covenant, God's holy Torah. Although the final terms of the covenant had not been fully spelled out, the people were called upon to make a choice and they voluntarily chose compliance:

So Moses came and called for the elders of the people, and laid before them all these words which the LORD

---

[593] Genesis 17:10-11.

[594] Genesis 17:14.

[595] As an aside, it was not uncommon for the vassal to be obliged to agree to the terms of the covenant, prior to those terms being revealed to him. More on this in a moment.

commanded him. Then all the people answered together and said, "All that the LORD has spoken we will do." [596]

In the Book of Deuteronomy, Moses reminds Israel of the blessings of obedience and curses for disobedience, prior to their anticipated conquest of the Promised Land. He concludes with this sobering warning, even giving them a hint as to how they should respond:

I call heaven and earth as witnesses today against you, that I have set before you life and death, blessing and cursing; therefore choose life, that both you and your descendants may live... [597]

In this Suzerainty Covenant, God's continued favour was contingent upon Israel's obedience.

Back to Corporate Solidarities

We're not told what would have happened to God's royal grant to the descendants of Abraham had he declined to observe the covenant sign of circumcision. But as head of the promised nation – as their corporate solidarity – we can speculate that God's blessing *may* have been revoked.

Moses was called to lead Israel to Mount Sinai and beyond. He would be the corporate solidarity for Israel under the Torah Covenant. As a descendant of Abraham, presumption of Moses' circumcision was a given. However, Moses failed to comply with the covenant seal upon his son Gershom. This

[596] Exodus 19:7–8a.

[597] Deuteronomy 30:19.

would have proven fatal, had not Moses' wife Zipporah intervened:

> *And it came to pass on the way, at the encampment, that the LORD met him and sought to kill him. Then Zipporah took a sharp stone and cut off the foreskin of her son and cast it at Moses' feet, and said, "Surely you are a husband of blood to me! So He let him go.*[598]

Had Moses defaulted on the sign of the Abrahamic Covenant, he would have been disqualified as Israel's leader under the Torah Covenant. For, under the Torah, Moses was to be Israel's corporate solidarity.

Original Sin?

Augustine of Hippo[599] was a Christian philosopher of the third and fourth centuries CE, whose ideas profoundly influence Christian thought to this day. He came up with the doctrine of Original Sin, which is to say that all human beings are sinful, inheriting their wicked nature from Adam. On that basis, little newborn babies are wicked sinners and desperately in need of Christian baptism lest they perish and end up in *Limbus Infantium.*[600]

---

[598] Exodus 4:24-26a.

[599] It was a place in modern Algeria – he wasn't a hybrid creature.

[600] Faced with the concept of unbaptised babies burning in hell for eternity, the Roman Catholic church invented a place, *Limbus Infantium,* where these unfortunate youngsters could spend forever. It wasn't heaven and it wasn't hell. It was like being in, well, limbo. They also came up with *Limbus Patrum,* which was for saints of the Old Testament (so called). That is, until Jesus came and rescued them. And you can't really argue with fact like that, can you?

Little babies cannot possibly be sinful – for which of God's holy commandments have these little mites breached? Babies are merely selfish, and that's out of necessity to ensure their survival. However, Adam is the corporate solidarity for mankind and there is a sense in which his sin has become ours. The proof of that statement is that we have inherited from him – not sin – but mortality. If a little child were to spend its entire life free from transgression of any of God's laws, he or she would still die – sooner or later. Death is what we have inherited from Adam, our corporate solidarity. As the Apostle Paul wrote in his first letter to the assembly at Corinth:

For as in Adam all die...[601]

The Noachide Laws

In his mercy, God made a covenant with all the descendants of Noah. Judaism deduced seven laws for gentiles from this covenant, summarised in Talmud as follows:

Our Rabbis taught: seven precepts were the sons of Noah commanded: social laws;[602] *to refrain from blasphemy, idolatry; adultery; bloodshed; robbery; and eating flesh cut from a living animal.*[603]

---

[601] 1 Corinthians 15:22a.

[602] The expression 'social laws' means the obligation for gentile societies to establish a judicial system.

[603] b.*Sanhedrin*.56a. It doesn't sound all that difficult until you stop and think about each of the six prohibitions. Just for starters, the ban on idolatry – the worship of false gods - would exclude a large percentage of today's gentile humanity from enjoying God's favour.

We might say that Noah is the corporate solidarity for gentiles. He is the significant individual to whom gentiles belong, noting that Jews voluntarily accepted a different (and more complex) covenant at Mount Sinai.

In summary (and to put it another way), all mankind are born 'in Adam' as their corporate solidarity. Jews are the exception, in view of their later covenant with God. Jews are 'in Moses'. Gentiles, subject to the Noachide laws are 'in Noah' if you like.

Who is Israel's Corporate Solidarity?

Clearly, there have been many significant individuals leading God's chosen people since the time of Moses. and within the communities, countless numbers have been *tsaddiqim* (righteous according to Torah). Yet the promised blessings of God have not yet been showered upon Israel in accordance with those promised through Moses in Deuteronomy.

The Apostolic Writings make the assertion that Yeshua is Israel's corporate solidarity. Study of the gospels reveals that Yeshua's life parallels the history of Israel in many ways. For example, in Matthew's narrative, Yeshua was supernaturally called out of Egypt to the Promised Land as a result of persecution:[604]

---

[604] In this case, the persecution had been directed at Yeshua (while still a toddler) in Judea and, following the death of Herod, Yeshua and his family were able to return.

*Now when Herod was dead, behold, an angel of the Lord
appeared in a dream to Joseph in Egypt, saying, "Arise, take
the young Child and His mother, and go to the land of
Israel, for those who sought the young Child's life are
dead."* [605]

A few verses previously, Matthew had made an
extraordinary statement about the family's flight to Egypt:

*When he arose, he took the young Child and His mother
by night and departed for Egypt, and was there until the
death of Herod, that it might be fulfilled which was spoken
by the Lord through the prophet, saying, **"Out of Egypt I
called My Son."*** [606]

Matthew is citing the words of Hosea chapter eleven (first
verse) which is **not a prophecy** and, in its context in the
Tanakh, has nothing to do with Yeshua. Critics of the
Apostolic Writings pounce on this fact in denouncing their
credibility. However, Torah declares Israel to be God's
firstborn son:

*Then you shall say to Pharaoh, 'Thus says the LORD: "Israel
is My son, My firstborn."'* [607]

Matthew is arguing that Yeshua — referred to in the Apostolic
Writings as the 'son of God' is the new Israel — that is, Israel's
corporate solidarity.

---

[605] Matthew 2:19-20.

[606] Matthew 2:14-15, emphasis mine.

[607] Exodus 4:22.

As the corporate solidarity Yeshua, having departed from Egypt, replays the Red Sea crossing through his baptism in the River Jordan. He is immediately tested in the wilderness for forty days – one day for each of Israel's years of wandering. Returning from the wilderness he duplicates Israel's experience at Mount Sinai as he gives his famous Sermon on the Mount, in which he raises the bar[608] on Torah-observance. He does this by contrasting compliance with the letter of the law with the more difficult 'spirit' of the law which reveals the heart of God behind the commandment. Here's one example:

> *"You have heard that it was said to those of old, 'You shall not commit adultery.' But I say to you that whoever looks at a woman to lust for her has already committed adultery with her in his heart."*

Which is easier? To avoid the actual commission of adultery or to avoid the private sin of lustful desire?

Yeshua himself claimed to be Israel's corporate solidarity in a slightly cryptic way:

> *I am the true vine...*[609]

The vine (or the vineyard) is an image of Israel found in several scriptures in the Tanakh. For example, when God is pleading his case against Israel through the prophet Jeremiah:

---

[608] Yes, *raises* the bar.

[609] John 15:1a.

Yet I had planted you a noble vine, a seed of highest quality. How then have you turned before Me into the degenerate plant of an alien vine? [610]

A study of the gospels proves that Yeshua kept Torah to the standard that he demanded of others. That is, he kept both the letter of the Torah and the spirit of the Torah in every circumstance. [611] In doing so, according to the Apostolic Writings, Jews who enter into covenant with God on the basis of Yeshua's actions as corporate solidarity are considered to have kept Torah perfectly and are entitled to all the blessings that God promised Israel at Mount Sinai for their compliance with Torah.

So, What's the Bottom Line?

The bottom line is that one of Yeshua's functions was to keep Torah perfectly – the perfect Jewish *tsaddiq* – on behalf of Israel. As the corporate solidarity (true Israel, if you prefer) he earned the promised blessings of the Sinai Covenant for Israel as a free gift. [612] The fine print is that for Jews to partake

---

[610] Jeremiah 2:21 also 12:10ff; Isaiah 5:1ff, 27:2ff; Ezekiel 17:5ff; Psalm 89:9ff.

[611] By 'Torah' I mean the written instructions. Generally speaking, he also observed the oral Torah, except where he perceived it was at odds with the spirit of the Torah. An example would be when he healed a man with a deformed arm on the Sabbath (see Matthew 12:9-13; Mark 3:1-5; Luke 6:6-10). The oral law permitted this only when a life was endangered.

[612] Yes, my Christian brothers and sisters, Yeshua came first and foremost *for Israel.* Yes, he was the antitype (fulfilment) of many prophetic pictures in Tanakh – the Passover lamb who secured Israel's redemption; the various sin offerings plus the goat for Azazel who bore Israel's sin; the bronze serpent who brought healing to the people of Israel who had fallen victim to the serpent's bite – to name but a few. These were historical events interwoven with Israel's identity. The inclusion of gentiles is simply an adjunct in God's salvific plan for Israel.

of this gift they are obliged to embrace him as their Messiah ben Yoseph, who will return as Messiah ben David at the conclusion of this age.

My Jewish readers are free to reject this concept, obviously. I simply ask that they see it as having some merit as a Jewish idea. I suspect that most of my gentile readers will have been (until now) totally unaware of the corporate solidarity notion. I ask that they also give it some consideration and reject the absurd Christian teaching that Yeshua kept Torah to free others from having the obligation to do so – that he abrogated Torah. I'm sorry, but that is nothing more than unbiblical nonsense.

That's really about all I have to say on Yeshua and trinitarianism. In the final and brief part of this book, for those readers still with me, I want to summarise the things we've discussed by way of a conclusion.

Are we there yet? Almost...

Part Six:
Jumbo Jettison?

What was it all about, Ezri?

The aim of this book, written for Jews and Christians, was to enable rapprochement by examination of the things that divide both parties who worship the God of Abraham, Isaac and Jacob. We likened those divisive issues to three elephants of varying size.

The smallest of the three was comprised of things which have arisen over the centuries, primarily as the result of misunderstanding. The little elephant need not exist at all – he really should vanish into thin air with a puff of smoke, ne'er to raise his little prehensile trunk again.

The middle-sized one was the issue of whether Yeshua of Nazareth's candidacy for the title Messiah was valid or void. The major problem has been the Christian church's failure to understand the Jewish expectations of the messianic role. Yeshua fulfilled a handful of those prophetic hopes – from a Christian perspective he was the Messiah Son of Joseph – but certainly not all of Israel's aspirations. Correctly understood, Messiah the Son of David has yet to make his appearance on the world stage. When he does come, he will raise the dead, sort out all this world's issues and rule in righteousness and peace from Jerusalem.

The only non-negotiable difference between Jews and Christians should boil down to the name of this exalted figure when he comes. If it's Yeshua, Christians are right; if it isn't, Jews are correct. This historically insurmountable obstacle should really be a divergence of opinion on the messianic moniker: you say 'עַגְבָנִיָּה'; we say 'tomato'.

To my Jewish friends I say:

> "Don't associate the name of Yeshua with the atrocities that have been committed in his name over the last two millennia. He was actually a very nice chap and if you ever do read the Apostolic Writings, you will find a lot of his teaching was stuff that you already accept as true and consistent with that of the sages. Shame the same can't always be said for his devotees."

To my Christian friends I say:

> "Try to put yourselves in Jewish shoes. [613] Imagine having to deal with Christian missionaries and their 'zeal without knowledge' attempts to persuade you that you're doomed to spend eternity in agonising torment, when all you want is for them to let you practise your own faith, as your forebears have done for thousands of years. Please my brethren and sistren, just love the Jews. If you want to have any serious religious discussion with the Jewish people, you must *earn* the right to do so."

---

[613] Actually, my cousin owns a shoe shop in St Kilda East called נַעֲלַיִם יְהוּדִיּוֹת and he can do a very special price for you. Just mention my name, okay?

Finally, there was what I perceive to be the biggest elephant of all, the Christian dogma of the Trinity. I presented an alternate approach – that the Apostolic Writings present Yeshua as the Memra in human form. This may (or may not) be more palatable to my Jewish friends even if it earns me the scorn of my Christian ones. But at least it is more consistent with the Second Temple Jewish mindset than with the classic trinitarian view, rooted in ancient Greco-Roman thought as it is.

What's the Bottom Line at the Bottom?

Whether you're a Jew or a Christian, if this book has helped you to understand the other mob's stance a little better, it has been worth the effort of writing it. Please don't leave it at that, though. Make the effort to befriend someone on the other side of the fence and invite them to endure this treatise as well.[614]

If enough folks do that, we might just be a little kinder to one another and be better prepared for what the future holds if, as I suspect, Islam – the major politico-religious force in the Middle East and North Africa increases its dominance in Europe and perhaps elsewhere as well.

If your opinions haven't shifted even a micron, then I still thank you for persevering to the end. That is a courtesy not often extended to those with whom we totally disagree. I also thank you for not starting a new whingers' group; #michaeloffendedmetoo.

---

[614] I'm not trying to generate sales. I authored another book, about twenty-five years ago (based on the convictions I held at that time). I have thrown every single cheque for royalty payments that I've received in the rubbish bin. Yes, true.

And so I finish this not–particularly–impressive chronicle in the same way that I began:

I authored this book for Jews and Christians, because of my sincere love for both groups.

The LORD bless you and keep you;
The LORD make His face shine upon you,
And be gracious to you;
The LORD lift up His countenance upon you,
And give you peace.[615]

---

[615] Numbers 6:24-26.

www.ingramcontent.com/pod-product-compliance
Lightning Source LLC
Chambersburg PA
CBHW031945080426
42735CB00007B/267